THE ZULUS

Text by
IAN KNIGHT
Colour plates by
ANGUS McBRIDE

First published in Great Britain in 1989 by
Osprey Publishing, Elms Court, Chapel Way,
Botley, Oxford OX2 9LP,
United Kingdom.
Email: osprey@osprey-publishing.co.uk

Also published as Elite 21 *The Zulus*
© Copyright 1989 Osprey Publishing Ltd.
Reprinted 1991, 1994, 1995, 1996, 1998, 1999

ISBN 1 85532 942 5

Filmset in Great Britain
Printed through World Print Ltd, Hong Kong

Acknowledgements
My principal debt is to that great Natal expert on
Zulu history and custom Mr. Sighart Bourquin. Over
the years 'SB' has been unfailingly generous with his
time, knowledge and hospitality. Without his help this
book would not have been written. *Ngiyabonga baba!*
My thanks also to Mrs. J. F. Duggan and the staff at
the Killie Campbell Library for their help and co-
operation; to Brian Maggs and Keith Reeves for
allowing me to use material from their collections: to
my patents for their support and encouragement; to
Dr David Rycroft for his advice on matters of
translation; and finally to Claire Colbert for her
priceless help with the photographic work.
This book is dedicated to Felicity.

Cover photographs courtesy of Ian Knight.

FOR A CATALOGUE OF ALL BOOKS PUBLISHED BY
OSPREY MILITARY, AUTOMOTIVE AND AVIATION
PLEASE WRITE TO:

The Marketing Manager, Osprey Direct USA,
PO Box 130, Sterling Hts, MI 48311-0130
UNITED STATES OF AMERICA
Email: info@OspreyDirectUSA.com

The Marketing Manager, Osprey Direct UK,
PO Box 140, Wellingborough, Northants, NN8 4ZA,
United Kingdom
Email: info@OspreyDiret.co.uk

VISIT OSPREY'S WEBSITE AT:
http://www.osprey-publishing.co.uk

The Zulus

The People

'A very remarkable people, the Zulu', the British Prime Minister, Benjamin Disraeli, said on hearing of a fresh disaster in the war of 1879. 'They defeat our generals; they convert our bishops; they have settled the fate of a great European dynasty'. Remarkable, indeed, to have taken on the full might of the British Empire at its height, and won, if not the war, at least some of the battles. Who were the Zulus, and how did they achieve the fame as warriors which they enjoy to this day?

The area now known as Zululand lies on the south-eastern coast of Africa, between the Drakensberg Mountains and the Indian Ocean. It is steep rolling grassland, dropping from cool inland heights to a sub-tropical coastal strip, and intersected by many river systems which have, in places, cut deep, wide gorges. In the valleys thornbush grew luxuriantly, and many of the heights were thickly forested. Until decimated by 19th century hunters, both black and white, the countryside teemed with game—antelope, wildebeest, elephant and lion. Above all, the area was covered with a wide mix of grasses which, with the comparative absence of tsetse fly, made it some of the best cattle country in southern Africa.

Cattle played a crucial rôle in the Zulu scheme of things, not just as a practical asset—a source of food and hides—but also as a means of assessing status and worth. Although African Iron Age deposits have been found across Zululand dating back to the 6th century, the Nguni people, the cultural and racial group to which the Zulu belong, wandered into the area in search of new pastures some time in the 17th century. They spread out over the countryside, slowly peopling it with clan groups who traced their origins to a common ancestor. Oral tradition has it that a man named Zulu established his homestead on the southern bank of the White Mfolozi River in about 1670. The name

Zulu man in everyday dress, carrying both a throwing and a stabbing spear, and—in his right hand—a round-headed knobkerry club of polished wood. His loin-covering is of strips of twisted fur. (Brian Maggs)

Glossary

This is a glossary of Zulu *military* terms; some words have alternative non-military uses, but for clarity we have used only the translation relevant to this book. Proper names are not included here, nor are they italicised in the body of the text. (Source: James Stuart Archive, ed. J. B. Wright and C. de B. Webb.)

amasi ....thick curdled milk

ibandla ....tribal council

ibheshu ....cowskin buttock flap

ibutho,
    pl. amabutho ....age-group guild, thus regiment

ikhanda,
    pl. amakhanda..........military garrison base

iklwa ....large stabbing spear

impi ....(1) body of armed men (2) war

i'mpondo zankhomo.....................'beast's horns' formation (see *uphondo*)

induna,
    pl. izinduna...............senior military or civil leader

ingxotha ....brass forearm band

inyanga,
    pl. izinyanga ....doctor

iphovela,
    pl. amaphovela ....headdress of stiff cowhide

isangoma ....diviner, 'witch-smeller'

ishoba,
    pl. amashoba ....tufted ends of cow tails

isicoco...........................ornamental headring

isifuba...........................centre ('chest') of Zulu army formation

isigaba ....group of associated *amaviyo* companies within regiment

isigodlo ....royal or command residence within a garrison

isihlangu ....large war shield

isijula ....long-bladed throwing spear

isiphapha ....broad-bladed throwing spear

iviyo,
    pl. amaviyo...............company within a regiment

iwisa ....knobkerrie, war club

izikhulu,
    sing. isikhulu ....elders, councillors

ka ....son of

palane............................outsize regiment

udibi ....teenage boys who acted as warriors' servants

umbhumbuluzo ....reduced-size war shield

umkhonto ....spear

umkhumbi....................circle of warriors gathered for orders

umncedo.......................genital sheath

umqhele........................fur headband

umthakathi,
    pl. abathakathi ....wizard, witch

umutsha ....fur groin flap

umuzi,
    pl. imizi.....................homestead, village

uphondo,
    pl. izimpondo............of Zulu army crescent formation

utshwala ....Zulu beer

Zulu means 'the heavens', and his followers took the name *amaZulu*, 'the people of the heavens'.

At this time the Zulus were no different from their neighbours. They lived in a series of village homesteads (*umuzi*; plural *imizi*) which were basically family units. Each village consisted of a number of huts built in a circle around a central cattle enclosure, and surrounded by a stockade. They were usually built on a slope facing east. The huts themselves were dome-shaped, like old-fashioned beehives. They were made by thatching grass to a wooden framework; the floor inside was made of polished clay, and a raised lip marked out the central fireplace. There was no chimney—the smoke escaped as best it could through the thatch. The layout of an *umuzi* reflected social relationships. The Nguni were polygamous, and a man might have as many wives as his wealth and status would allow. He himself lived at the top of the homestead facing the entrance with the wives and children of his senior house to the right, and those of the subordinate house to the left. Any dependants lived at the bottom, near the gate.

Daily life for the men consisted of tending the cattle and performing the heavier tasks around the homestead. Cultivation of cereal crops, and all household duties, fell to the women. Since beasts were too precious to slaughter merely for food, meat was only eaten on special occasions; the staple diet was curdled milk—*amasi*—and maize, augmented sometimes with pumpkins and sweet potatoes.

These vegetables were grown in small plots near each homestead. The grain was stored for use all year round in large wicker baskets raised on stilts to keep them away from the damp and rats, or in an underground pit sealed with a large stone. For diversion the Zulus had *utshwala*, a thick, rather sour beer; and tobacco, which was dried, crushed and taken as snuff. In general the people lived a healthy, outdoor life—they were neither as markedly tall or short as other African peoples, and in complexion they were, on average, rather light skinned.

Their utensils, the Zulus made of wood, bone, clay, basket-weave and iron. Iron ore was scattered in easily accessible surface deposits across the country, and particular clans gained high reputations as smiths—notably the Mbonambi near the coast, and the Chube in the dark Nkhandla forest overlooking the spectacular Tugela River. It is no coincidence that both these areas are rich in ore and fuel. The smith smelted the ore in a shallow pit, over which a fire was lit. Bellows made of cowhide sacks pumped by hand were used to feed in air via clay nozzles. Once the ore was melted, it was extracted and hammered into shape. Like many African peoples, the Nguni regarded this process with superstitious awe, the more so because the best

Characteristic 19th-century domed 'beehive' huts, typical of both *amakhanda*—garrisons—and ordinary homesteads. These examples have been built by archaeologists over the surviving clay floors of King Cetshwayo's *isigodlo* at Ulundi.

Zulu blacksmiths at work: a famous sketch from the 1840s by George French Angas. The smith works the bellows while his assistants retrieve the ore from the furnace and hammer it into shape. (British Museum)

smiths were said to temper their products with human fat. The smiths made hoes and, of course, spears.

Weapons and Costume

Early spears had a small, leaf-shaped blade with a long shank or tang. Having forged his blade, the smith turned it over to another specialist, the spear-maker. He selected appropriate wood for the shaft, and drilled out the end with an awl. Strong vegetable glues were used to fix the blade in place, and this was bound with a wet fibre. When this was dry, the join was sealed with either split cane, or with a tube of hide cut from a calf's tail. The Zulu word for a spear is *umkhonto*, although there are several different spears, each with its own particular function. The *isiphapha*, for example, was a broad-bladed spear and was used for hunting game; the *isijula* was used in warfare.

For his everyday protection in a wild country, a man would carry a spear and *iwisa*, a knobkerrie made of hardwood with a large polished head. He would also carry a small oval shield made of cowhide, reinforced with a stick held in place by a double row of hide lacing. The top of the stick was usually decorated with a strip of civet or genet fur, wound round.

A man would remain at his father's homestead until he married, when he would establish an *umuzi* of his own. The change in status was considerable and indicated by means of the headring, or *isicoco*, donned by men immediately prior to their first marriage. The *isicoco* was a fibre sewn into the hair, plastered with gum and polished with beeswax. In the 19th century it was fashionable to shave the crown and back of the head, leaving just the hair around the ring. Occasionally the ring was raised up on a pad of hair. Young unmarried men would sometimes tease out their hair and build it up into bizarre shapes with clay and tallow.

Ordinary costume was minimal. A man was required to wear an *umncedo*, a sheath of plaited grass and leaves; with this, he would be considered adequately dressed in all company. However it was usual to wear a loin covering over this: a thin strip of hide around the hips, with an oblong of soft dressed cowskin low on the buttocks (*ibheshu*), and strips of fur (*umutsha*) at the front. Fur from the civet, genet and samango (green) monkey were the most popular types, but sheepskin and antelope were sometimes used. Often two or more skins would be twisted together to resemble tails. Samango monkey tails were sometimes worn either side of the *ibheshu*. Only chiefs were allowed to wear a cloak of leopard skin, with leopard claws as a necklace. Chiefs often carried sticks with carved wooden heads as staffs of office.

Clothing for married women consisted of a large pleated leather skirt. The hair was also worn in a distinctive fashion: a small circular patch was teased out, coloured with red ochre and the head shaved round it. This is the origin of some of the extravagant headdresses which can be seen among married women in Zululand today. Unmarried girls wore a fringe of brown strings low on their hips, or a small leather skirt. Minimal as this was, it always seemed to protect their modesty, as several British officers commented to their chagrin.

Most Zulus loved to ornament themselves. Before the 1840s beads were the prerogative of an important few, but with the arrival of European traders they became very common. Both men and women wore them, particularly unmarried girls, who wore them in strings around the arms and legs and slung around the body. Ingots of brass, perhaps traded from the Portuguese in the north, were worked to produce highly-prized heavy rings, worn around the neck and arms. Both sexes pierced their ears and wore large plugs in the lobes. These were made of ivory, bone, clay and later of sugar-cane. Men often carried snuff-spoons in their ears, or tucked into their headrings. Such spoons were dished at one end and tapered to a point at the other—sometimes two or three such points—which were used to scratch the head. The snuff itself was carried in gourds, horns, or wooden containers from a thong around the neck.

Witchcraft and Warfare
The Nguni lived in great dread of the evil effect of witchcraft, and often wore magical charms— necklaces with special blocks of wood and pouches with magical medicine—to ward off evil. If someone had an accident, or was injured by a wild animal or in war, they would turn to the *inyanga*, a medical doctor who carried a wide range of herbal remedies and poultices which were often effective. If, however, the problem was beyond the skill of the *inyanga*, it was thought to be the work of *abathakathi*—wizards—who could only be identified by the *isangoma*, or diviner.

The Nguni believed that ancestral spirits watched over their everyday lives, and that misfortunes were either the result of spirits being offended, or of witchcraft. The *isangoma* was able to

A Zulu man carrying a knobkerry; note the twisted-fur loin flap, and the headring marking his status as a married man. (**Radio Times Hulton Picture Library**)

7

decide these matters. Ancestral spirits could usually be propitiated by sacrificing a beast, but wizards would have to be 'smelt out' in a grim ceremony. Both men and women could be *isangomas*, but women were thought to have particularly acute powers. They wore their hair in braids, and were dressed in bizarre costumes, slung around with magical charms; they carried gnus' tails as the badge of their profession. At a smelling-out

A Zulu man dressing a friend's hair. Both wear the *isicoco* headring of married men; the one on the left has shaved his head all round the ring, the one on the right has grown the hair below the ring but shaved the crown—both common 19th-century styles. This picture may date from *c.*1865. (Killie Campbell Africana Library)

ceremony the suspects would sit chanting in a circle whilst the *isangoma* danced and capered around them. At last, she would strike one with the gnu's tail. This was an accusation which brooked no defence, since even an innocent man might be possessed by *abathakathi* without his knowledge; and the penalty was a gruesome death. A sharpened stick about 18 in. long was driven into the victim's anus. This was the Nguni judicial sanction extreme; ordinary criminal cases were tried before a chief, and a fine in cattle was the usual penalty, although serious offenders might be clubbed to death.

Until the 19th century warfare in Zululand was infrequent and largely bloodless. When disputes did

arise, often over grazing rights, the combatants would meet at an appointed time and place, with the women and children turning out to watch. Individual warriors would step out and challenge rivals from the opposing forces to individual combat. Amidst much jeering and cheering, spears would be thrown, and a few casualties sustained. One side would eventually withdraw. It seems likely that, with plenty of unclaimed pasture, a defeated clan could simply move on to find new lands. However, by the late 18th century the

Two married women, probably of King Mpande's court, sketched by Angas; they wear the traditional married woman's long skirt, but not the top-knot of hair also associated with this status. The baskets and gourds are typical Zulu utensils. (British Museum)

population was such that Zululand was becoming congested, and it was no longer possible for clans to have access to good grazing all the year round. Historians still argue the point today, but it seems likely that this competition for natural resources was the cause of the shattering violence which was to follow.

9

Shaka and 'The Crushing'

The Zulus played little part in this early conflict; they were a minor clan living between two more powerful neighbours, the Mthethwa of King Dingiswayo to the south-east, and the Ndwandwe of King Zwide to the north. Oral tradition has it that Dingiswayo was a wise and just ruler and Zwide a treacherous despot; this may be a case of history being interpreted by the victors, but Zwide does seem to have been the more ruthless, attacking and subduing his northern neighbours.

Then history introduced a new factor, with all

A young Zulu man with his hair shaped into a fantastic crest with clay and tallow—an extreme example of a common practice. He also wears a snuff-spoon through his pierced earlobe, and snuff containers round his neck. (S. Bourquin)

the elements of a dark fairy-story. Sometime in 1786 Chief Senzangakhona of the Zulu met a maiden of the eLangeni clan named Nandi, when she was fetching water by a pool. They became lovers; but, when Nandi became pregnant, the Zulu chief's advisors sent her away, saying she was harbouring an *i-shaka*, an intestinal parasite. When she was subsequently delivered of a son Nandi called him Shaka. Senzangakhona was resentful of the responsibility forced upon him, and soon found a reason to drive Nandi and her son away. They ended up among the Mthethwa, where Shaka grew to manhood, and duly enlisted in the Mthethwa army.

It was customary for youths of about 17 to be banded together into guilds, called *amabutho* (sing. *ibutho*), for the ceremonies attendant upon the onset of manhood. The *amabutho* were required to perform duties for the chief, and Dingiswayo used these age group guilds as a basis for military units. Shaka joined the Mthethwa iziCwe *ibutho*, and seems to have found an outlet for his personal frustrations in battlefield aggression. He was not, however, impressed by the style of warfare then practised—he preferred to charge down upon his enemy and engage him in hand-to-hand combat. He found the light throwing spears too flimsy for this purpose, and designed his own broad-bladed spear for close combat. It had a blade about 18 in. long by $1\frac{1}{2}$ in. wide, set into a stout haft 30 in. long. With typical gallows humour, he called it *iklwa*—the sound it was said to make on being withdrawn from a deep body thrust.

Shaka's reputation as a ferocious warrior drew him to Dingiswayo's attention, so much so that when Senzangakhona died in 1816 the Mthethwa chief put Shaka forward as his candidate for the Zulu throne. The legitimate heir was discreetly disposed of.

Shaka called up all the available fighting men—a total of perhaps 400—whom he organised into four regiments grouped according to age, thus completing the militarisation of the *amabutho* system. They were armed with copies of the *iklwa*, and given new, large war shields, called *isihlangu*, which covered them from shoulder to ankle. It had been customary for men to wear hide sandals: Shaka considered these awkward and ordered his men to discard them; to harden their feet they were required to stamp flat heaps of thorn-bush.

The warriors were trained in a new tactical formation, the *i'mpondo zankhomo*, or 'beast's horns'. One body, the *isifuba* or 'chest', rushed down on the enemy in a frontal assault, whilst flanking parties, the *izimpondo* or 'horns', rushed out on either side to surround them. A further body, the 'loins', was kept in reserve. When they reached the enemy the warriors were supposed to hook the left edge of their shield over the edge of their opponent's, and wrench to the left. This dragged the opponent's shield across his own body, throwing him off balance, and preventing him from using his own spear arm; it also exposed the left side of his body to the Zulu *iklwa*.

Shaka tried out his new army on his neighbouring clans. It was brutally effective. The Zulus had begun their rapid and ruthless rise, a period still known as *mfecane*—'the crushing'.

Gqokli Hill

The sudden emergence of a new power allied to the Mthethwa on his very border was a problem for Zwide of the Ndwandwe. In 1818 he collected an army and moved against Shaka. In less than two years Shaka's army had grown to perhaps 4,000; it was heavily outnumbered by a Ndwandwe host of 8,000 to 10,000, but the Zulu had superior training and weapons.

Shaka took up a position on a rocky knoll known as kwaGqokli, which crested a spur running down to the White Mfolozi River. A jumble of boulders and coarse grass, Gqokli is a tough climb; and a slight shoulder on the summit provides a depression, out of sight from the lower slopes, in which Shaka could hide his reserves. The battle took place some time in April 1818, and began with Shaka attempting to reduce the odds. Small parties of Zulus defended the river crossing, disrupting the Ndwandwe approach, and a large herd of cattle was used to lure further enemy troops away from Gqokli. The Ndwandwe commander then tried repeated frontal attacks on Shaka's warriors, who were drawn up in lines around the summit of Gqokli. These were unsuccessful; the Ndwandwe,

still wearing sandals, still throwing their spears, were taken aback by the fierce close-quarter combat of the Zulus. Finally, the Ndwandwe formed up into a column and attempted to punch a hole through the Zulu lines. With perfect timing, Shaka unleashed his hidden reserves, who streamed out to surround the Ndwandwe column, smashing it in a few minutes' brutal mêlée. The Ndwandwe army began to disintegrate and, although a running fight developed which lasted most of the day, the Ndwandwe finally withdrew.

An *inyanga*, or practitioner of traditional medicine. He carries his remedies in an assortment of horns, gourds and other containers slung around his neck and in the bag in his hand. *Izinyanga* used natural medicines with a degree of success, aided by the faith of their patients. (Brian Maggs)

An *isangoma* or diviner of supernatural phenomena. Although there are suggestions of European influence in her dress, this picture does convey something of the *isangoma*'s intimidating appearance. The braided hair, inflated bladders in the headdress, and above all the gnu's tail in her right hand are all traditional badges of her calling. (Royal Engineers Museum)

Gqokli hill was the supreme vindication of the new Zulu tactics; and in the immediate aftermath Shaka consolidated his position by snapping up further clans. A prize plum fell into his lap when Dingiswayo mounted his own campaign against the Ndwandwe, only to fall into Zwide's hands and be put to death. In an ironic reversal of the tactic which had brought him to power, Shaka quickly put forward his own candidate for the Mthethwa throne, and absorbed Dingiswayo's former empire. This was too much for Zwide, who reorganised his troops along Zulu lines, and made an all-out bid to crush the Zulu upstart.

The Second Zulu/Ndwandwe War of 1819 was a turning point in the history of Zululand and, indeed, of black South Africa. The Zulu were once more heavily outnumbered, and Shaka chose to retire before the Ndwandwe advance, taking his cattle with him and emptying grain stores. Since all Nguni armies lived off the land, this caused serious problems for the Ndwandwe. After a week of fruitlessly chasing the Zulus through some of the most rugged parts of the country, the Ndwandwe began to retire. As they crossed the fords of the Umhlatuze River, Shaka launched his attack. The fighting raged over a wide area, and at the end of it the Ndwandwe were smashed. His kingdom shattered, Zwide himself escaped with part of the clan and settled in the eastern Transvaal district. Those who remained behind were killed by Shaka, or incorporated into the Zulu state; sections of the Ndwandwe army which survived in cohesive units fled to the north, where their commanders were able to carve out small empires of their own.

The destruction of the Ndwandwe removed the largest obstacle to Shaka's power. He turned his attention to clans living on his western and southern borders. In a series of campaigns between 1819 and 1824 he dislodged powerful groups living in the Drakensberg foothills and south of the Tugela River. Many were completely wiped out; others were driven over the mountains into the interior, or to the south. Some, chiefs like Mzilikazi of the Khumalo, and Matiwane of the Hlubi, became rootless marauders on the high veld, attacking all they came across. Others ended up as refugees amongst the Mpondo and Xhosa tribes on the fringes of the British Cape Colony. Large tracts of land were completely depopulated.

At the centre of it all, the new Zulu state went far beyond anything Zwide or Dingiswayo had envisaged. The clans incorporated into the Zulu state retained their identity but their chiefs were subordinate to Shaka, who often killed off the legitimate ruler and raised up a junior member of his family, who therefore owed his position directly to Shaka. Nguni chiefs were traditionally advised by a council called the *ibandla*, consisting of the *izikhulu*, or 'great ones' of the nation. Important clans within the Zulu state had representatives within the *ibandla*, but visitors to Shaka's court were horrified at the regularity with which Shaka had his advisers killed: they may not always have been men of the highest rank, but it was a brave man on the *ibandla* who would question the king's policies. The effect was to take power out of the hands of the traditional chiefs and invest it in the state. Military and civil state officials were called *izinduna* (sing. *induna*), and were appointed by Shaka himself. There was an element of meritocracy in this—even commoners could become *izinduna* if, for example, their skill in war brought them to Shaka's notice.

Army Organisation

The army was a crucial element in the system. It is difficult to arrive at reliable figures for the strength of Shaka's army, but if it was 400 in 1816, 4,000 in 1818, and a maximum of about 15,000 when the great phase of expansion ended in 1824, its rapid growth is evident. The *amabutho* continued to be organised on an age basis, with youths of the same age being recruited from all the clans across the country. This reduced the risk, in such a conglomerate kingdom, of too many men from the same clan dominating a regiment, and being a potential source of dissent. Each *ibutho* was between 600 and 1,500 strong, and they were quartered in barracks known as *amakhanda* (sing. *ikhanda*), literally 'heads', which were strategically placed about the kingdom to act as centres for the distribution of royal authority. The *amakhanda* themselves were civilian homesteads writ large: there was a circle of huts around a central open space which served both to contain the regiment's cattle and as a parade ground. They were surrounded by a stockade, sometimes a formidable barrier consisting of two rows of stakes leaning inwards so as to cross at the top, with the gap in between filled with thorn-bush. At the top of each *ikhanda* was a fenced-off section known as the *isigodlo*, where the king or his representatives would live when in residence. Each regiment had its own *induna* appointed by the king. In some cases female members of the king's family were placed in charge of *amakhanda*.

In Shaka's time the vast majority of warriors were unmarried. This had less to do with channelling warriors' frustrated sexual energies into military aggression (as the Victorians suggested) than with maintaining control over military resources. Whilst unmarried the warriors were, in effect, subject to whatever national service the king might dictate: when they married they were allowed to disperse, establish their own homesteads, and give their first allegiance to their families and clan chiefs. By prolonging bachelorhood artificially, Shaka kept his army at full strength. This was not as uncomfortable for the warriors as it may seem, as Zulu moral codes provided perfectly acceptable outlets for sex outside marriage.

As unmarried men with no resources of their own, the warriors were dependent on the king's bounty. The vast numbers of cattle looted in Zulu raids were the property of the state, but the king quartered them with his regiments, who were allowed to use their milk products. Morale within the Zulu army was extremely high: the common age of the warriors, their extremely successful record, and the terror this inspired among neighbouring

The only contemporary portrait of King Shaka kaSenzangakhona, sketched by one of the Europeans who first visited his court. His appearance has been somewhat romanticised—note the size of the spear, and its elaborate head—but does tally in basic particulars with other descriptions. (Killie Campbell Africana Library)

In a scene reconstructed with some accuracy for the TV drama series '*Shaka Zulu*', Shaka trains members of Chief Dingiswayo's *iziCwe* regiment in the use of his newly-invented stabbing spear; note the combined use of the shield with an under-arm spear thrust. (SABC/Emil Wessels)

peoples, combined with the material benefits—in terms of gifts of cattle—which proceeded from a successful expedition, all led to a high *esprit de corps*. Since the *amabutho* looked to the king for patronage, this further strengthened the position of Shaka himself.

Organisationally each *ibutho* was divided into two wings, led by *izinduna*, and sub-divided into companies, *amaviyo*. Each *iviyo* numbered roughly 50 men. In addition, some regiments were partially divided into *isigaba*—groups of *amaviyo* who were particularly associated with each other for one reason or another. When the king established a new *ibutho* and granted it a herd of cattle, he would select beasts with a particular uniformity of hides. From these would be made the war shields, and each regiment therefore had its own distinctive shield colour. War shields were the property of the state, not the individual; kept in raised stores in each *ikhanda*, they were issued at the start of each campaign. The *isihlangu* shield might be as much as 50 in. long and 30 in. wide, individual warriors picking out shields which suited their personal height. In Shaka's time the shield colours were meticulously adhered to, the difference between particular colours often being quite subtle: e.g., an *ihwanqa* shield was black with white patches all over

it, while the *impunga* shield was the same, but the patches were less clearly distinct. In general the most senior regiments carried white shields, and the youngest black, with all grades for regiments in between, although dun-coloured, red and grey (black and white hairs intermixed) were also carried.

War regalia

Each regiment also had its own uniform of feathers and furs. The bushy parts of cows' tails (*amashoba*) were worn in such profusion as to almost cover the body completely. They were worn in dense bunches, suspended from a necklace, falling to the

Shaka's 'tactical edge': the Zulu stabbing spear, *iklwa*. The exact specifications varied, although these are typical. The tang fitted into the bored haft and was secured by glue and bindings. (Author's collection)

King Dingane's residence, emGungundhlovu, partially reconstructed as a set for 'Shaka Zulu'. The original complex had a larger circumference and an inner palisade, but this does give a fair impression of the appearance of an *ikhanda*.

waist at the front and the knees at the back. They were worn around the elbows and knees, and sometimes from the wrists and ankles. A kilt made of golden civet and green samango monkey pelts, carefully twisted together to resemble tails, was worn over the ordinary *umutsha* by some senior regiments. A headband called *umqhele* was worn: made of leopardskin for junior regiments, and otterskin for senior ones, it was stitched into a tube, stuffed, and neatly tied at the back of the head. Oblong earflaps of samango skin for most warriors but occasionally of leopardskin, hung down either over the cheeks, or sometimes on either side of the back of the head. On to this basis were fixed the plumes granted to each individual *ibutho*.

There is very little direct surviving evidence relating to specific Shakan regiments, but certain conventions were followed. Young regiments, for example, usually wore the long grey tail feathers of the sakabuli bird. These were either worn in a dense bunch, attached to a plaited grass framework which fitted on to the top of the head; or in plumes on either side of the head, tied to quills and tucked inside the headband, so that the plumes pointed out and back. Blue crane feathers were a sign of seniority, worn either at the front of the head, or in ones and twos on either side. The young regiments often wore *amaphovela*, a grotesque headdress consisting of two stiff horns of cowhide standing upright above the temples, the bottoms sticking out below the headband, and with either small tufts or

whole cowtails attached to the tips, the latter falling back down the head. Ostrich plumes were worn in great profusion at the front, back or sides, sometimes sticking out at all angles. The black/white imagery was continued, young regiments having more black ostrich feathers, senior ones more white. In addition, the king might grant particular plumes to regiments who distinguished themselves, and small bunches of the scarlet feathers of the lourie bird were given as rewards for bravery to individual warriors. Other similar symbols of bravery were a necklace of interlocking wooden beads, and *ingxotha*—a brass armband, rather like the cuff of a gauntlet, worn around the right forearm.

Theoretically, each warrior was supposed to provide his own uniform, and if it was not up to scratch he was likely to be mocked and thrashed by his fellows. In practice, however, the huge expansion of the army during the *mfecane* far outstripped the capacity of Zululand's wildlife to costume it, and feathers and pelts were obtained either as tribute or by trading with other parts of southern Africa, notably Thongaland in the northeast. There is a certain amount of evidence to suggest that in Shaka's time a good deal of this costume was worn into battle; the more expensive and fragile items would probably have been left at home in the *ikhanda*, however.

Shaka's personal war dress is said to have consisted of a kilt of civet and monkey skins, with a collar of the same material, and white cow tails around the elbows and knees. Around his headring he wore a headband of otterskin into which were tucked bunches of lourie feathers tied to thorns. At the front he wore a single long crane feather. His shield was white, with one black spot on the centre right face.

A young Zulu warrior, photographed in the 19th century; the bulk of Shaka's warriors were unmarried men such as this. This man is probably not a member of the Zulu king's army, and wears no regimental regalia, although his shield is about the right size and is appropriately coloured black. (S. Bourquin)

The army on campaign

Before a regiment set out on campaign it was doctored by an *isangoma* who specialised in preparations for war. The warriors would be sprinkled with magic potions, and required to chew a piece of meat which had been specially prepared. Often they had to drink a potion which made them vomit. The intention was to bind them together and make them invulnerable to enemy weapons. The king might call up two regiments, and order them to challenge one another to see who would excel in the coming fight. Warriors would step out from the ranks and *giya*—proclaim their own virtues, act out their past deeds of valour, and challenge warriors known to them in the rival regiment; bets would even be laid. After the fight, Shaka would call up the same regiments, and the challenges would be recalled, though the bets were not called in. Those who had particularly distinguished themselves would be rewarded, and those accused of cowardice executed.

When an army set out on campaign it began in a single column, but then split into several columns. As it neared enemy territory it sent out an advance guard of men from each regiment, who made no attempt to conceal themselves but acted as aggressively as possible, hoping to convince the enemy that they were the main body. They were preceded by a screen of scouts who did conceal themselves, and who were expected to note every detail of the enemy's movements. Shaka's military intelligence system was renowned for its efficiency. Once the enemy was spotted, the army (or *impi*, the name for any body of armed men) was formed into an *umkhumbi*, or circle, and given final instructions for the attack. For most of his reign Shaka accompanied his armies in person, and was undoubtedly the most able commander of his generation. Once the attack had been launched the Zulu commanders watched the battle from high ground, issuing orders by runner or hand signals; by this stage, however, it was usually very difficult to recall an attacking force.

After the battle was over there were certain ceremonies to perform. Any man who killed another in battle was required to disembowel the corpse of his victim. This was not gratuitous mutilation: it was believed that the spirit of a dead warrior was in his stomach, and if it was not released he would haunt his slayer, visiting all manner of misfortune upon him until he eventually drove him mad. It must be admitted, however, that the tension of combat was sometimes vented on enemy dead. The victorious warrior was also supposed to dress himself in the clothing of his fallen opponent, and wear it until he had performed certain cleansing ceremonies at his personal *umuzi*. For this reason Zulu armies often disbanded after a successful battle, and there was a limit to the prolonged campaigning which even Shaka could make them endure.

Provisioning the army was another problem. At the start of the campaign the warriors were accompanied by *udibi*—boys too young to fight—who were allocated to individual warriors, often relatives, as personal servants to carry sleeping mats and food. These boys only accompanied the army on the first day of march, however, returning to their homes after that. In Shaka's day this was

An *induna* or military commander, painted by Angas. His shield is smaller than that of the warrior in the background and is probably for dancing rather than for war. He wears bunches of scarlet and green lourie feathers on either side of his head, a badge of rank or distinction. The beads around his neck suggest a festive occasion. (British Museum)

enough to see the *impi* beyond the Zulu borders, since Shaka expected his troops to cover up to 50 miles a day, and beyond that the *impi* had to forage for its own supplies. If Shaka rationalised this situation at all, he no doubt believed that it was another incentive for his *amabutho* to be successful in their raiding.

Both the Zulu state and the army were highly centralised, and needed a dynamic personality at their head to keep them functioning—especially in the early years, when there was no inherited weight of tradition. Shaka was certainly dynamic. Though many accounts of his bloodshed have been grotesquely exaggerated, there is no question that the lives of his individual subjects meant nothing to him, and that he drew no distinction between the interests of the state and his own personal wishes. He waged war to the death; and at his court a flick of his wrist would consign a man to the executioners for no more weighty crime than making him laugh when he wanted to be serious, or interrupting his speech with a sneeze. He maintained an iron grip on his empire, and as a general he was unsurpassed; only towards the end of his life did his judgement falter and his behaviour become increasingly psychotic.

The Coming of the Whites

On Christmas Day 1497 the Portuguese explorer Vasco de Gama noted in his log the existence of a stretch of African coastline which he named *Terra Natalis* in honour of the birth of the Lord; it was to be over 300 years before there was any further European interest in the area, but the area south of Zululand was to remain known as Natal.

The first whites to play a rôle in Zulu history arrived at the bay of Port Natal—later Durban—in 1824. They were a party of traders, hunters and adventurers led by two ex-Royal Navy lieutenants, James Saunders King and Francis George Farewell; their aims were to explore the commercial potential of links with the Zulu state. To reach Shaka's kingdom they had to travel through miles of depopulated countryside, and when they arrived the Zulu king took pains to impress them with the

One of a remarkable trio of photographs of Chief Ngoza ka Ludaba, taken in about 1865. Ngoza was chief of the Majozi, a section of the Chube clan, who broke away during the reign of King Mpande and settled in Natal. In this view he wears simple everyday costume limited to the *umutsha* groin-flap. (Africana Museum, Johannesburg)

power and wealth of his kingdom. It is true that the whites probably played only a very minor rôle in Shaka's affairs; none the less the Zulu king does seem to have been intrigued by them, granting them title to the land around the Port, and questioning them closely about the British colonies beyond the fringes of his own sphere.

Shaka was particularly interested in the European way of making war. He was fascinated by the 'Brown Bess' muskets carried by the party, and insisted on a demonstration; when a lucky shot fired by one of the sailors dropped an elephant, he was suitably impressed. He constantly demanded that the whites join him on his expeditions, and on several occasions they did so.

They also had the opportunity to witness Shaka's last clash with the Ndwandwe. In 1826 Zwide's successor moved down from the Transvaal in an attempt to regain his old lands. Shaka mustered his army and marched north-west, confronting the Ndwandwe at Ndolowane Hill. One of the whites' servants was ordered to fire several times into the Ndwandwe ranks, after which the Zulus charged. Twice they were repulsed; but at last the Ndwandwe gave way, and the Zulus slaughtered them.

In general, however, Shaka's policy looked increasingly southward. He moved his personal capital from kwaBulawayo ('the place of killing') to Dukuza in Natal, and established an *ikhanda* not far north of the Port. In 1828, much to the embarrassment of the whites, he sent a diplomatic mission to the Cape Colony. At the same time he sent his army on a raid which harried the Mpondo on the very fringe of British territory. His exact purpose is not clear; in any event the mission was coolly received, and Shaka was angry at its failure. When the army returned he sent it straightaway on a raid to the north.

It was a move that showed uncharacteristic lack of judgement. The army was exhausted, and Shaka was alienating his power-base. The majority of the Zulu people were weary of Shaka's increasingly erratic behaviour and the frequent summary killings. In September Shaka's half-brothers Dingane and Mhlangana seized their moment, and pounced on the king as he sat largely unattended, receiving a delegation from another tribe. They stabbed him to death with the spears of his own invention. Dingane immediately seized the throne. When the army returned—defeated for once—it was relieved to escape Shaka's wrath.

Dingane

King Dingane was very different in character from his predecessor, and had different problems to contend with. He lacked Shaka's zest for military expansion, and his reign was characterised by a need to keep together the state system which, under Shaka, had not had time to mature. The first problem was securing his own position. Personal favourites of Shaka were killed, and Dingane re-organised the army. Several of Shaka's *amabutho* were allowed to marry and disperse, and the remnants of others were re-organised into new regiments. Dingane then called up youths of an appropriate age and started enrolling new regiments dependent on his personal patronage. Initially he did not send his army on campaign; but the defection of a large section of the nation, the Qwabe clan of Chief Nqetho, who simply crossed the Tugela and fled to the south of Natal, persuaded him to adopt a more aggressive policy towards his neighbours. The Ndebele (Matabele)—an embryonic state under construction in the Transvaal under the leadership of Mzilikazi, a refugee from Shaka—particularly attracted Dingane's attention, although fighting was inconclusive.

Natal was another problem. The original European settlers had either died or moved on, but

Ngoza in full regalia, with young warriors. Although not the uniform of an *ibutho* of the Zulu king's army, since the clan had split away, this does show many characteristic items of Zulu 'full dress'—note the *amaphovela* and *isakabuli* feathers in the young warriors' headdresses. The size of the larger *isihlangu* shields is very evident here. (Africana Museum, Johannesburg)

they had been replaced by an increasing group—mostly elephant hunters—who proved quarrelsome and scheming. Dingane wished to remain on good terms with whites, but watched with apprehension as once-empty Natal began to fill up with blacks—survivors of Shaka's raids returning to their lands, and political refugees fleeing from Zululand. These people placed themselves under white protection, and formed the nucleus of a black population hostile to Zululand on its very borders. This was a situation which ultimately undermined the absolute authority of the Zulu monarch, since it sapped his army's strength and gave a safe refuge for dissidents.

Indeed, it was from Natal that the threat to Dingane's kingdom was to come, but it came from an unexpected source: the arrival of a new group of whites—the Boers.

The Boers, or Afrikaners, were descendants of Dutch, French and German settlers at the Cape who, in the 30 years following the British occupation in 1805, had become so disgruntled under British rule that they were prepared to leave. In 1834 a reconnaissance party had reported that

Natal was excellent cattle country and largely under-populated; in the mid-1830s Boer families packed their possessions into ox-wagons and began the movement known as the Great Trek. In 1836 they did what Dingane had failed to do—they drove Mzilikazi out of the Transvaal. In 1837 some of them crossed the Drakensberg and set up temporary camps in the Natal foothills.

Their arrival disturbed Dingane. There is little doubt that he felt their huge herds, military skill in African warfare, and lack of respect for native chiefs were a serious threat to the stability of his kingdom. Dingane entered into negotiations with the Trekker leader Piet Retief, and finally agreed to cede him part of Natal. But when Retief and 70 of his unarmed followers attended Dingane's residence at emGungundhlovu on 6 February 1838 for a celebratory dance, Dingane suddenly leapt to his feet and cried out 'Slay the wizards!' The Trekkers were overpowered and dragged to Dingane's place of execution, where they were clubbed and impaled.

The next day Dingane mustered his army and despatched it against the Boer encampments in Natal under the command of Ndlela kaSompisi of the Ntuli clan, one of the men who had risen through the ranks of Shaka's army. The subsequent campaign was a crucial test for the Zulu army: for

Ngoza in war dress, with members of a senior *ibutho*; note the headrings, padded otterskin headbands, and single crane feathers worn by these middle-aged warriors. These photos are probably virtually unique as a record of the appearance of authentic Zulu regimental costume of the period. (Radio Times Hulton Picture Library)

A fascinating photograph, apparently taken early in the 20th century; the original caption unfortunately does not record the occasion, but this may well be a group of surviving veterans of King Cetshwayo's army. The warriors in the centre have similar headdresses and shields, suggesting an old *ibutho* uniform. The two on the outside have bunches of *isakabuli* feathers on top of their heads; the rest have large bunches of lourie feathers on either side. The man in the centre is clearly a chief, and carries a staff, as well as a small bag of magical charms with his shield. (Brian Maggs)

the first time it would have to face firearms in large quantities. The Boers had perfected offensive tactics involving firing from horseback, and the defensive circle of wagons known as the *laager*. The Zulus, however, consistently refused to be overawed by guns, and commanders such as Ndlela showed great tactical ingenuity in countering Trekker tactics.

The Zulu attack fell upon the foremost encampments on the Bushmans and Bloukranz Rivers on the night of 16/17 February. Dawn was the traditional time for a Zulu attack—it caught the enemy unawares, when the spirits are lowest, yet gave sufficient light to direct the attack. On this occasion it is probable that this practice was abandoned in the hope of catching the Boers unprepared, when they could not use their guns effectively. The night attacks were partially successful: the leading Boer parties were wiped out, but survivors escaped in the confusion and were able to warn camps further back. Several put up a spirited defence and drove the Zulus off. Even so, the Boers lost nearly 300 of their men, women and children dead, and a further 200 of their servants. The Zulus also took most of their cattle.

Yet the attack had failed in its purpose of driving out the Trekkers, and Dingane no doubt realised a counter-attack was inevitable. When it came, however, it proved surprisingly easy to repulse. On 6 April a party of 347 mounted men led by Piet Uys and Hendrick Potgeiter set out towards emGungundhlovu; four days later they spotted a huge herd of cattle near eThaleni Mountain, and advanced to round it up. It was a trap: as many as 6,000 Zulus, concealed in long grass and on nearby heights, swept down, scattering the Boer forces and killing Uys himself.

For the British traders at Port Natal the war proved a dilemma. Dingane had sent them messages assuring them he meant no harm, but they felt morally obliged to side with fellow whites. They

Young warriors step out from the ranks of their regiment to *giya*—proclaim their own praises, and boast of the feats they will perform in the coming battle—part of the ceremony of mustering the Zulu army for war. (Author's collection)

were also tempted by the possibility of looting some of Dingane's cattle. In April, therefore, 18 of the settlers raised an army of around 4,000 Natal blacks, and crossed into Zululand in support of the Trekkers. They got as far as the *ikhanda* of 'Ndondakasuka on the Zulu side of the Tugela when, on 10 April, they ran into a Zulu *impi*. Many of the Natal levies were armed with rifles, and the battle raged back and forth; but at last one flank of the settler army collapsed, and the Zulus were able to complete their encircling movement and drive the settlers back, pinning them against the river. Only four settlers escaped, and hundreds of their levies were killed. The Zulus followed up their success with a raid which swept through Natal, destroying the whites' huts at the Port. So far, in their first conflict with whites, the Zulus were winning hands down.

The tide turned in August. Dingane made one more attempt to exterminate the Boer camps in the Drakensberg foothills. By now most of the Trekker families had collected in a large laager of over 200 wagons on the Bushmans River. Between 13 and 15 August as many as 10,000 Zulus repeatedly attacked the position. On one occasion they used the cover of a *donga*, a dry watercourse, to advance

within a few yards and fling throwing spears over the wagons into the laager. Shaka had outlawed throwing spears, but Dingane had re-introduced them apparently in an attempt to counter Boer firepower. Since a spear could be thrown with some accuracy for up to 50 yards, while an average rifle of the time was not very effective beyond 100 yards, there was some logic in this. On another occasion the Zulus tried to set fire to the wagons with spears wrapped in burning straw. These attempts were uniformly unsuccessful, however, and the Zulus were eventually forced to retreat.

Blood River

In November 1838 a new leader, Andries Pretorius, joined the Boer laagers, and the Trekkers went on to the offensive. Pretorius organised a 'commando' of around 470 whites and 340 black or Coloured servants, accompanied by 64 wagons and at least two small cannon, and set out on 3 December. On the 14th they ran into a Zulu advanced guard; on the 15th they drew up in a laager on the banks of the Ncome River. The site of the laager was carefully chosen, so that one side was protected by the river and another by a *donga* which flowed into it. Wooden gates were used to block the gaps between each wagon, and the horses and oxen were brought within the circle. Lanterns were tied to whip-stocks and raised over the wagons to hinder any Zulu attack under cover of darkness.

They attacked at dawn. In fact, daylight caught Ndlela with his force divided. He had to cross the Ncome to attack the laager, but while his left horn was in position, the chest and right horn were still drawn up on the hills overlooking the Zulu bank. The left horn was supposed to remain out of musket range until the rest of the army had crossed, but as soon as the light was clear they rose to their feet and charged. A few yards from the wagons they were met with a heavy volley, and forced to retire. They tried the same manoeuvre several times without success. Bodies of warriors then broke away to occupy the deep *donga*, where they could mass only a few yards from the wagons. Pretorius ordered a sally, which lined the lip of the *donga* and fired down into the Zulus, who were too cramped to reply with their spears. Ndlela finally managed to get his chest and right horn across the river; but it was impossible to control them, and the regiments frittered themselves away in unco-ordinated attacks. At last the Boers rode out and chased them from the field. The Zulu reserve tried to restore the situation, but the Boers caught them as they crossed the drifts. So many Zulus were forced into the river that it became choked with corpses and stained blood-red. The Ncome has been known as Blood River ever since.

The defeat at Blood River was a catastrophe for Dingane, but it did not destroy the Zulu state. Pretorius advanced to emGungundhlovu and

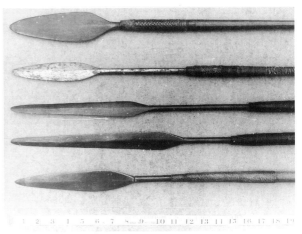

A selection of throwing spears. Outlawed by Shaka, these were re-introduced during the reign of Dingane, perhaps because they offered a potential counter—however inadequate—to Boer musketry. The three in the centre date from the 1879 war. (Author's collection)

found it in flames, the king fled. The bodies of Retief's men still lay on the hill of execution, and the treaty ceding Natal was found in Retief's wallet. When a party from the commando tried to round up cattle beyond the White Mfolozi on 27 December it walked into a repetition of the eThaleni trap, and only just escaped.

The Voortrekkers withdrew, and opened negotiations with Dingane to end the war. The Trekker terms were that Dingane should abandon southern Zululand and move north. This he agreed to do, and even sent his eMbelebele regiment to build a new homestead in what is now southern Swaziland; the Swazi, however, resisted, and Dingane's plan was frustrated. His final downfall came about when his half-brother Mpande defected to the Boers with a large section of the army. Mpande had been thought a harmless simpleton, but this facade hid a shrewd political mind. The Trekkers agreed to acknowledge Mpande king of the Zulus, and to provide military support, in return for peace and land in Natal.

In fact, the Boers took little part in the subsequent fighting. Mpande's army confronted Dingane in the Maqongqo Hills in northern Zululand. Though the Boers were hardly engaged, their presence was enough to give Mpande the edge, and Dingane was defeated. He fled with a few loyal retainers to the territory of Chief Sambane of the small Nyawo clan. In a fit of rage, he had Ndlela killed for losing the battle. Dingane did not long

The arrival of the Boers in the 1830s brought a technological challenge which the Zulus were not equipped to meet. The combined use of horse and gun, and the defensive wagon laager, proved difficult to overcome. This is the reconstructed laager on the battlefield of Blood River. (Author's collection)

survive him—Sambane conspired with the Swazis to have him killed. The exact details of his death are uncertain, but one story has it that he was set upon one morning as he crawled out of his hut. This was in March 1840; on 10 February Pretorious had already proclaimed Mpande king of the Zulus.

Mpande and Cetshwayo, 1840–1878

Both the personality and reign of King Mpande have been much misunderstood. It is true that he was vain, and enjoyed the pleasures of his court life, but Mpande's apparent indolence concealed the deep political perception of a born survivor. He had, after all, remained alive under both Shaka and Dingane, when so many of his family had been assassinated as potential rivals. He was to rule for over 30 years—longer than the other kings put together—and to die a natural death. He not only managed to hold the kingdom together in the

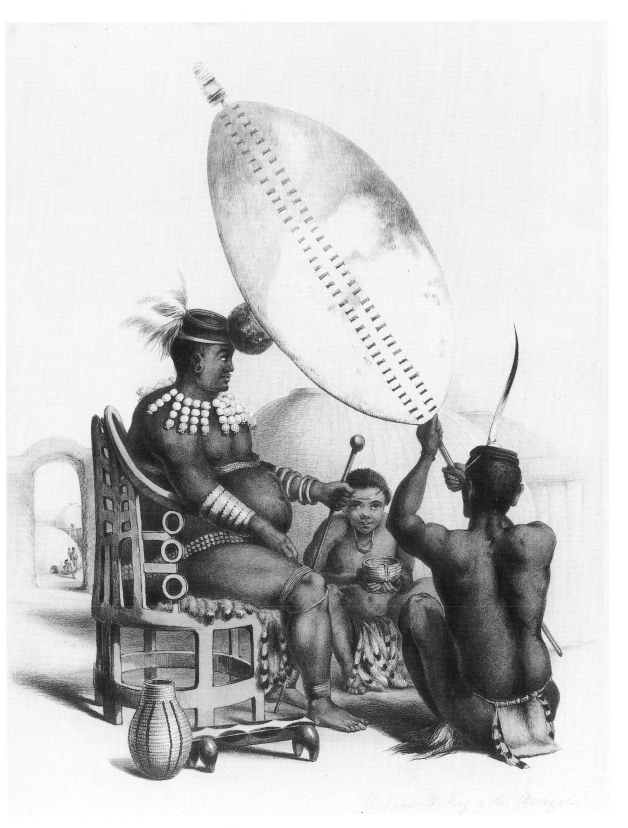

King Mpande kaSenzangakhona; a famous portrait by Angas which captures the king's deceptively indolent appearance. On hot days his attendants would hold a shield to protect him from the sun. Note the *ingxotha* on Mpande's right arm. (British Museum)

A group of warriors photographed at King Cetshwayo's 'coronation' in 1873. Several regiments are represented, and the men seem to be wearing war dress—a simplified form of ceremonial regalia—and carrying the *umbhumbhuluzo* shield. (Killie Campbell Africana Library)

aftermath of the Trekker and civil wars, but consolidated its position during years of menace from growing European colonies on its borders.

The two years of conflict between 1838 and 1840 were a disaster for the Zulu kingdom. The dead and wounded amounted to several thousands, and the army was shattered by the civil war. Individual chiefs had exacted a high price in personal power in exchange for supporting Mpande, and many who were dissatisfied with the state of affairs in Zululand moved to Natal. In addition, the Boers took 30,000 head of cattle as the price of their help in defeating Dingane, and laid claim to land as far as the Black Mfolozi—two-thirds of the kingdom itself. Fortunately, in 1842 Britain decided to exercise its claim to Natal; after a sharp fight at Port Natal the Trekkers withdrew for the most part to the Transvaal, and their claims to Zulu territory lapsed. The southern borders of the kingdom became accepted as the Tugela and Buffalo Rivers.

Nevertheless, the reign of Mpande, and to some extent that of his son Cetshwayo, were marked by an attempt to re-establish the central authority of the Zulu state. Mpande's position was precarious, since he needed the support of the *izikhulu*, the great chiefs who made up the *ibandla* council, and could no longer afford to intimidate them as Shaka had done. Although the king continued to exercise the power of life and death over his subjects, the more despotic elements of Zulu kingship were gone for good.

Natal posed an ever-increasing threat to Zulu security. From the depopulated wastelands witnessed by Farewell in Shaka's day, the black population of Natal had grown to 100,000 by 1845, and 305,000 by 1872. In the 1850s as many as 4,000 a year were leaving Zululand. When, in 1843, Mpande tried to consolidate his position by attacking rival members of his own household, an aunt, Mawa, simply fled to Natal with 3,000 of her followers. Why were they leaving? Some, like Mawa, were fleeing the king's justice; but many went because, with the increase in the numbers of whites in Natal seeking workers, life there offered more potential for cattle and wives than the Zulu army. In the 1850s one estimate put the total strength of Mpande's *amabutho* as low as 6,000. Nevertheless, the king patiently revised the state system and gradually rebuilt his authority.

This process suffered a set-back in the 1850s. Mpande, unlike his predecessors, had a number of sons, but was unwilling to weaken his own position by naming his successor. His eldest son, Cetshwayo, had considerable support amongst the *izikhulu*, but the king himself favoured his next eldest, Mbuyazi. Both princes had military experience, and were popular within their respective regiments. Each began courting chiefs and *izinduna*, and each developed a faction—the iziGqoza of Mbuyazi, and the uSuthu of Cetshwayo. The king tried to avoid conflict by keeping the princes at opposite ends of the country, but in November 1856 the iziGqoza fled to the Tugela River and Mbuyazi tried to appeal to the Natal authorities for support. It was not forthcoming, but the white hunter and trader John Dunn offered support in a private capacity. Cetshwayo called together his own supporters and, on 2 December 1856, attacked the iziGqoza at 'Ndondakasuka on the banks of the Tugela, not far from where the Port Natal settlers had been massacred in 1838. John Dunn's party fired volleys at the attacking uSuthu, and Mbuyazi's regiments put up a stiff fight; but the uSuthu numbers prevailed, and the iziGqoza were pinned against the river bank. When the fighting finished the victorious uSuthu massacred the iziGqoza; as many as 20,000 were slaughtered. Mbuyazi and several of Mpande's other sons were killed.

The victory at 'Ndondakasuka established Cetshwayo's claim to the throne beyond doubt. Mpande continued to rule, however, and the next decade and a half was marked by shifting internal allegiances. In September or October 1872 Mpande finally died and was buried at his royal *ikhanda* at Nodwengu on the Mahlabatini plain.

Cetshwayo persuaded the Colony of Natal to recognise his coronation the following August—support which would cost him dear in due course—but once enthroned he felt able to adopt a more rigorous policy than his father. He refused to negotiate with the Transvaal Boers over a border dispute which had been smouldering for ten years, and he tightened his control over the *amabutho*. The *izikhulu* remained powerful, however, and resisted attempts to re-centralise state power; it could, and did, veto the king's decisions, and the king's authority over several very powerful chiefs, like his half-brother Prince Hamu kaNzibe, and Zibhebhu kaMapitha of the Mandhlakazi section, remained tenuous. These divisions would come to the fore in the subsequent war of 1879.

The army had changed noticeably since Shaka's day. The majority of the warriors were no longer recruited from newly subject clans as in the days of military expansion, but through natural means. At the age of 14 or so each boy was expected to serve as an *udibi*; and at the age of 17 or 18 they would report to an *ikhanda* and *kleza*—drink milk direct from the udders of the king's cattle—accepting his bounty, and in return offering service to the state. They underwent a period of cadetship, looking after the king's herds and the royal homesteads. When there were sufficient numbers of them around the kingdom the king would call them together and form them into a new *ibutho*, ordering them to go and build their own *ikhanda* at a specified location. Occasionally a new regiment would be incorporated with an old one, or assigned to an existing barracks. The warriors were not, however, permanently mustered as they had been in Shaka's time: once the units had been established, warriors were allowed to spend long periods at home with their families while the *amakhanda* would be cared for by a skeleton staff. The king would call up a particular *ibutho* when he had need of it.

It is important to note that the duties of the

A watercolour by African artist Gerard Bhengu of one of the ceremonies of the *umkhosi* or 'first fruits' festival: the killing of a black bull by warriors of a young *ibutho*. (Killie Campbell Africana Library)

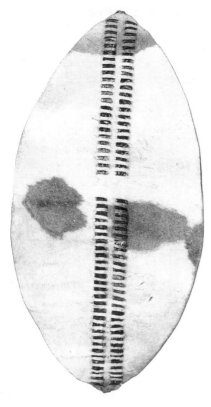

regiments were not, and never had been, purely military, although in Shaka's day there was more than enough campaigning to keep them busy. They were also the state workforce, and were required to work the king's fields, build new homesteads, organise hunts, and partake in the national ceremonies. The greatest of these was the *umkhosi*, the 'first fruits' or harvest festival, which took place every year in December or January. The king would give the order for his army to muster, and the *izinduna* at the various military centres would summon the warriors in their local areas. If an *ibutho* had its headquarters near the king's homestead—Cetshwayo established himself at oNdini, or Ulundi, on the other side of the plain from

A shield, white with red spots, from the Thulwana *ibutho*, taken from King Cetshwayo's residence at Ulundi after the battle of 1879. (Africana Museum, Johannesburg)

The two types of shield carried by the Zulu army from the 1850s: (left) the *umbhumbhuluzo* (here, 39½ × 19½ in.) and the *isihlangu* (here, 54 in. × 29 in.); the former lacks its fur crest, which has also been cropped off the edge of the photograph of the *isihlangu*. Both these examples date from 1879. (Author's collection)

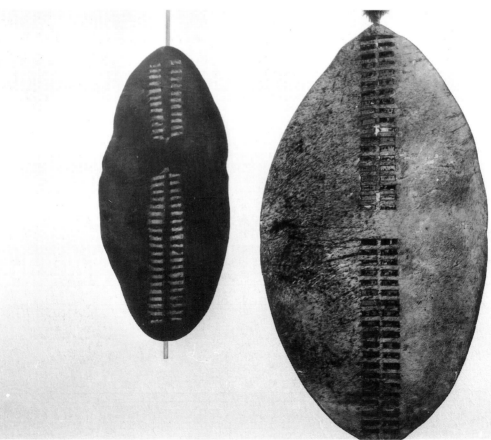

Nodwengu—it would be expected to muster within 24 hours. If not, the warriors would march to the capital by regimental companies from each district, and form up when there. The king would appoint them a place to camp. The ceremonies themselves included a binding together of the army, in which warriors of the youngest regiment present would have to kill a bull with their bare hands. The meat from the bull was then butchered and distributed amongst the *amabutho*.

Mpande had found it impractical to keep his young men unmarried for too long—they were tempted by the easy availability of wives in Natal—so the regiments married earlier. The prized white shields, once a symbol of élite unmarried regiments, became synonymous with married men. Indeed, both Mpande and Cetshwayo maintained *amabandhla amhlope*, 'white assemblies', who appear to have been a compromise between old and new systems, intended to prolong the active service of married men. These were married men permanently available to the king but who were allowed to live with their wives in an *ikhanda*, though even they were allowed to return to personal homesteads almost at will. The famous Thulwana regiment, Mpande's favourite—which had so many men of rank that it had a section known as the *inhlabamasoka*, 'the select ones'—was such a regiment in Cetshwayo's time, and lived at Ulundi itself.

Cetshwayo had some success in revitalising the *amabutho*, particularly the youngest regiments who owed him the greatest personal allegiance. The iNgobamakhosi, Cetshawyo's favourite, was a *palane* regiment of unusual size—perhaps as many as 6,000 strong. The uVe, formed shortly before the war in 1879, was 4,000 strong, and incorporated into the iNgobamakhosi. The flood of refugees had dwindled, and Cetshwayo cut down on the number of exceptions allowed to military service; he was therefore able to increase his army to about 40,000.

Tensions within the army sometimes reflected divisions within the state. At the first fruits ceremony in 1878 the Thulwana and iNgobamakhosi clashed, and some 60 warriors were killed. The fight had been sparked off by grievances over women taken as wives by a young section of the Thulwana, but it is no coincidence that the Thulwana were commanded by Hamu kaNzibe, who was widely thought to have resented Cetshwayo's ascendancy.

Another source of military manpower came from the abaQulusi, who were unusual in that they were essentially a regional, rather than age-grade regiment. They were descendants of an *ikhanda*, emaQulusini, established by Shaka near Hlobane Mountain in northern Zululand, who had settled in

A powder horn, apparently taken from a dead Zulu after Rorke's Drift; and (foreground) a wooden snuff container. (Keith Reeves)

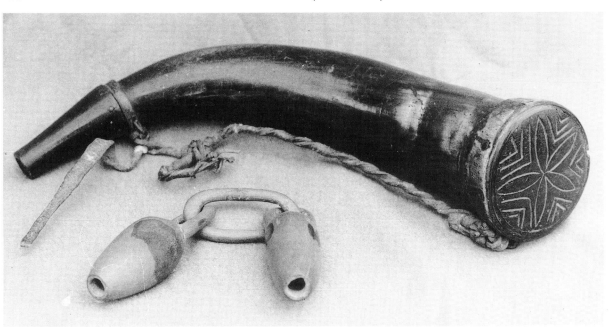

29

A remarkable pair of photographs, probably taken in 1873, showing a warrior in full regimental regalia. It is not possible to identify the *ibutho*, since sources for this period are incomplete and often contradictory. However, the components of full dress uniform are clearly visible: the extensive use of cow tails around the body, the earflaps and headband of leopardskin, and various plumes of the headdress. The shield is of the large *isihlangu* type. (S. Bourquin)

the same area when they dispersed and married. They mustered and fought as a state regiment, and were fiercely loyal to the king. There are references to an *ikhanda* still in use in the area in 1879.

There were differences, too, in the warriors' armament. In the 1850s Cetshwayo had introduced a new type of war shield amongst the uSuthu. Called *umbhumbuluzo*, it was about 3½ft long by less than 2ft wide. Cetshwayo considered that this was lighter and easier to wield than the *isihlangu* type. Both types were carried, however, even within the same regiment. It is possible that the *umbhumbuluzo* type was more popular with the younger warriors. The colour-coding of the shields, so precise in Shaka's time, had become less so by the 1870s. The

overall equation of black with youth and white with experience remained the same, but the positioning of patches and spots was less exact, and there were fewer variations of type. Although our knowledge of shield colours in the 1870s is imprecise, there seem to have been no grey or dun colours, and some *amabutho* seem to have had different shield colours within the same regiment—these may have reflected particular sections or companies.

Guns, too, were available to the Zulu army in large quantities by Cetshwayo's reign. They had first been taken from the Voortrekkers in the 1830s, and Mpande had tried to obtain them to strengthen his position against Dingane. When he later became king he demanded guns from white traders in an attempt to compensate for the weakness of his army. Gun-running from Natal was officially frowned upon, but did take place. It was a common practice for European powers to dump obsolete arms on the unsophisticated native market, and Africa had an inexhaustible demand. In the aftermath of the

Napoleonic Wars thousands of old 'Brown Bess' muskets bearing the Tower mark were sold cheaply in Africa, and with each new weapon that came into service the old makes would be sold off. The Zulus well appreciated their significance: after 'Ndondakasuka, John Dunn made his peace with Cetshwayo, who adopted him as his agent when dealing with whites. Cetshwayo wanted guns to secure his position within the kingdom, and Dunn purchased hundreds. Other important chiefs also had white traders who advised them, and who were a further source of supply. In addition, thousands of guns came into the Portuguese port of Delagoa Bay—as many as 20,000 in the 1870s alone. Most of these found their way into Zululand. Even rifles such as the Enfield, standard British issue in the 1850s and '60s, could be traded for as little as a sheep in the 1870s. If the quantity was sufficient, however, the quality was sadly lacking. Many of the guns were in poor condition, and the traders provided little back-up in terms of spare parts or even ammunition. Powder was of poor quality, percussion caps were in short supply, and pebbles were sometimes used in place of bullets. Nor was there anyone to train the warriors: individuals like Prince Dabulamanzi kaMpande and Chief Zibhebhu kaMaphita were recognised as good shots, but most warriors believed that the higher a gun was pointed, the further it would shoot, and many held the butt away from their shoulder to avoid the recoil. Battlefield accounts suggest the volume, not the accuracy, of Zulu fire.

The War of 1879

Lurid British accounts justifying the invasion of Zululand in 1879 portrayed it as a preventative campaign waged against a cruel and bloodthirsty despot and his army, a 'celibate man-destroying machine'. Most historians now accept this view as the propaganda it was, and suggest that the causes of the war lay rather in a British desire to simplify the complex political situation in southern Africa by joining the disparate British and Boer states together in a federation; a large independent Zulu state was seen as a threat to this scheme. In addition, many in the growing colony of Natal wanted to see Zululand opened to free trading and labour-recruitment, neither of which were possible when the king (in theory at least) controlled trade and Zulu manpower was fully utilised by the amabutho system. Minor border incidents which took place in 1878 were seized upon, and the British presented a stiff ultimatum to King Cetshwayo which demanded, among other things, the disbandment of the amabutho. The king himself and a number of his izikhulu were aware of the gravity of the situation; but feeling ran high within the army that the national honour was at stake, and the young regiments in particular refused to consider British demands. On 11 January 1879 the British crossed the border in three columns[1].

The king and his council considered their strategy carefully. It was not a war waged at their initiative, and Cetshwayo hoped to win political advantages by keeping the Zulu army within his borders: it would, therefore, be a defensive campaign. The British Centre Column, accompanied by Lt.Gen. Lord Chelmsford himself, was correctly identified as the most serious threat: the bulk of the army would be directed against this. Those men from the amabutho who lived in the coastal strip would report to the amakhanda there, and would be used to contest the progress of Col. Pearson's Right Column; the abaQulusi would try to check Col. Evelyn Wood's Left Column. The majority of the regiments were already at Ulundi, where they had gathered for the first fruits ceremony. They were doctored for war in the traditional way. A Sotho doctor from beyond the Drakensberg, renowned for his skill, was employed: he paid particular attention to guns. He burnt various medicines over a shard of pottery, and the warriors held their guns down so that the smoke wafted into the barrels, thus ensuring that they would fire straight and true. In the giya ceremonies, first the Khandempemvu (umCijo) and iNgobamakhosi amabutho vied against each other, then the Nokhenkhe and Mbonambi. Altogether this main striking arm totalled in excess of 20,000 warriors. Probably on 17 January, it marched off to confront Lord Chelmsford's army; and it encountered the British camped beneath a rocky outcrop known as Isandlwana.

[1]For a fuller account of the battles of 1879 see MAA 57, The Zulu War.

Isandlwana and Rorke's Drift

The king himself had not accompanied the army, which was entrusted to Chief Ntshingwayo kaMahole Khoza, who had a great reputation as a general, and Chief Mavumengwana, the son of Dingane's commander Ndlela. The army was in good spirits, but it should be noted that neither the *izinduna* nor the warriors had much combat experience, and· there were few who remembered Blood River 40 years earlier. Nevertheless, the commanders managed to lead the army undetected to within a few miles of the British camp where, on 22 January, it was discovered by a British patrol. The young regiments, particularly the Khandempemvu, immediately launched an attack without waiting for instructions. The battle which followed took place with very little direction from the Zulu high command.

The battle caught Chelmsford's force divided. Early that morning, in response to the increase in Zulu activity in the area, the general had taken roughly half his forces away from the camp at Isandlwana to search for the *impi*. He had left behind six companies of the 24th Regt., two guns, and a number of mounted volunteers and levies. The Zulu advance developed from some hills to the left of the camp, and caught the defenders scattered over a wide plain in front of the camp. The 24th opened up a heavy fire, and the Zulus facing them were pinned down; but as the traditional 'chest and horns' attack developed, the British were outflanked. They began to fall back on the camp and, encouraged by the shouts of their *izinduna*, the Zulus rose and charged after them. The fighting raged at close quarters among the tents and transport wagons and on towards the Natal border, the British standing back to back while their ammu-

Zulu smiths do not seem to have manufactured battle-axes, but they were acquired from tribes renowned for making them by trade, like the Pedi of north-eastern Transvaal. These typical examples are decorated with metal wire, introduced by European traders in the mid-19th century. (Author's collection)

The youth of Shaka, c. 1805
1: Nandi
2: Shaka
3: Mthethwa chief

A

3

1

B

2

The Battle of Gqokli Hill 1818
1: Warrior, Isipezi regiment
2: Ndwandwe commander
3: King Shaka kaSenzangakhona
4: Warrior, Fasimba regiment
5: Young Ndwandwe warrior
6: Warrior, Ndabezibona unit
7: Senior Ndwandwe warrior

7

AngusMcBride

Meeting between Shaka and Europeans, 1824
1: Lt.Francis Farewell
2: *Imbongi*
3: King Shaka
4: Xhosa interpreter

D

The court of Dingane, 1830s
1: Youth, dancing dress
2: King Dingane
3: Ndlela kaSompisi

E

Skirmish between Boers and Zulus, 1838
1: Boer Voortrekker
2: Warrior, Mbelebele regiment
3: Warrior, Kokoti regiment

F

The Battle of 'Ndondakasuka, 1856
1: Warrior, uDhloko regiment
2: Prince Cetshwayo kaMpande
3: Warrior, Impisi regiment

G

Warriors muster, 1870s
1: Zulu girls
2: Warrior, Mtuyisazwe regiment
3: Warrior, uKhandempenvu corps
4: *Udibi* boy

H

The court of Mpande,1870s
1: King Mpande kaSenzangakhona
2: Warrior; umXapho regiment
3: Warrior; iNdlu-yengwe regiment

Angus McBride

3

2

1

I

An *impi* is doctored for war, 1870s
1: *Isangoma*
2: Warrior, iNgobamakhosi regiment
3: Warrior, Thulwana regiment

J

The aftermath of Isandlwana, 1879
1: Warrior, Mbonambi regiment
2: Warrior, Indlondlo regiment
3: Warrior, iNgobamakhosi regiment

FOR NATAL

Angus McBride

3   2   1   K

The Battle of Mhome Gorge, 1906
1: Zulu rebel
2: Private,Durban Light Infantry
3: Constable,Zulu Native Police

nition held out, until at last they were overcome. Elements of the Zulu reserve pursued the few survivors; and about 4,000 men of the Thulwana, Dhloko, iNdhlondhlo and inDlu-yengwe *amabutho*, led by Prince Dabulamanzi, crossed into Natal and went on to attack the supply depot at Rorke's Drift.

The garrison there—B Company, 2/24th—had been warned of the Zulu approach by survivors of Isandlwana, and were able to barricade the two mission buildings with biscuit boxes and mealie bags from the supplies. Dabulamanzi's men assaulted the post from five in the afternoon until after midnight but, although they stormed one of the buildings, they could not dislodge the defenders. At dawn on the 23rd they called the attack off.

Isandlwana was a disaster of the greatest magnitude for Chelmsford, killing 850 of his white troops and 400 Natal blacks who had been recruited to fight their traditional enemy, and scotching his invasion plan. Hundreds of rifles fell into Zulu hands, with thousands of rounds of ammunition. Yet it had been a costly victory for the *amabutho*. Over 1,000 warriors lay dead around Isandlwana, with a further 400 at Rorke's Drift. The survivors tried to bury the bodies in *dongas*, ant-bear holes, or in the grain pits of nearby homesteads, but the numbers were so great that many had to be left on the field with just a shield to cover them. Warriors took rifles from the men they had killed, and stripped and disembowelled the dead. They then dispersed to their homes, taking their wounded with them—hundreds of men suffering injuries from heavy calibre bullets, which were beyond the skills of the *izinyanga*. The king was angry that many of the warriors did not report to Ulundi for the purification ceremonies, and appalled by news of the casualties. 'An assegai has been thrust into the belly of the nation,' he said; 'there are not enough tears to mourn for the dead'.

There was other fighting on the 22nd; an *impi* of between 4,000 and 6,000 warriors attacked Col. Pearson's coastal column on the march at Nyezane. The Zulu attack was premature however, and despite the vulnerability of the British columns when on the march, the warriors were unable to press home their attack. Over 300 Zulu bodies were found on the field. Pearson's column continued its advance to the deserted mission station at Eshowe, where it received news of Isandlwana and

King Cetshwayo kaMpande, photographed during his visit to Britain.

entrenched itself. The local *amabutho* contingents beseiged it.

The first phase of the war had gone Cetshwayo's way, although his inability to keep his army in the field made it difficult for him to exploit his advantage. It was March by the time he was able to collect together his army at Ulundi and, after careful discussion with his *izinduna*, decided to launch an attack against Evelyn Wood's Left Column. Since it had crossed into Zululand this had been engaged in constant cattle-raiding and skirmishing with the abaQulusi, and the followers of a renegade Swazi prince named Mbiline. It was undoubtedly the most dangerous of Chelmsford's surviving columns.

Hlobane, Khambula and Gingindhlovu
The new Zulu offensive coincided with fresh British activity. On 28 March Chelmsford had crossed the Tugela with a column intending to relieve Eshowe.

He gave orders to other British commanders along the frontier to make demonstrations to draw off the Zulus. On the same day Wood tried to clear the abaQulusi from their stronghold on Hlobane Mountain. Several parties of mounted volunteers scaled the summit, where a running fight ensued. At the height of the action, however, the main Zulu army from Ulundi came into sight. Such bad luck

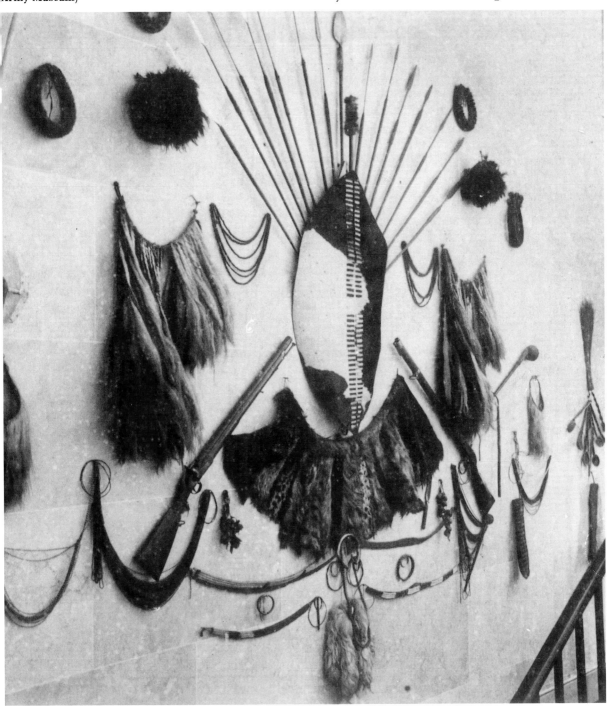

was appalling timing for the British, and it turned Hlobane into a débâcle as Wood struggled to extricate his troops. Those on the summit could only escape via a steep rocky staircase known as the Devil's Pass—over a hundred were killed. Wood fell back on his fortified base at Khambula Hill; the Zulus camped a few miles away that night, and the next morning advanced to attack Khambula.

The battle of Khambula was the most decisive of the war. Cetshwayo had learned from the stories of Isandlwana, and issued strict instructions that the *amabutho* were not to attack fortified positions, but to try to draw the British out from their earthworks. In the event, the Zulu right horn was in position before the chest and left, and a mounted British sortie was able to goad them into attacking. Wood's position consisted of a wagon laager and an earthwork redoubt; for over four hours the Zulus launched fierce but unco-ordinated attacks which several times penetrated the defences, but were unable to overrun them. At last they were chased from the field by mounted volunteers in a particularly savage pursuit.

Zulu losses at Khambula were comparable to those at Isandlwana, probably considerably greater. British burial parties noted that the young *amabutho* had suffered particularly heavily, and many *izinduna* and chiefs had died because they had exposed themselves to encourage their men. Border patrols noted the lamentations from homesteads across the river as word of the casualties spread to the civilian population. And there was more bad news for Cetshwayo: on 2 April Chelmsford's Eshowe Relief Column had been attacked by 12,000 warriors at Gingindhlovu.

Local elements of most of the main *amabutho* made up the *impi*, which was led by Somopho kaSikhala and accompanied by veterans of Isandlwana like Prince Dabulamanzi and Sigcwelegcwele kaMhlekehleke, fiery commander of the iNgobamakhosi regiment. Chelmsford had drawn his forces up in a square, protected by a ditch and

Members of the Natal Native Contingent 'mopping up' after the battle of Ulundi. The artist has captured the appearance of the different African groups well: the man on the left is a Swazi, who seem to have worn full regalia into battle. In the centre is a Natal African, wearing some items of European clothing and with a distinguishing red rag just visible tied round his head. The Zulu wears no regimental regalia. (Author's collection)

earth rampart, and the combined volley, cannon and Gatling fire cut the warriors down before their charges could strike home. The *impi* was scattered. Chelmsford relieved Eshowe and retired to Natal to prepare a new invasion.

Ulundi

The twin blows of Khambula and Gingindhlovu shattered Cetshwayo's strategic plans. The morale of the army was shaken, and it was clear that military victory was impossible. As Chelmsford began his new invasion in June the Zulu king stepped up his attempts to reach a diplomatic solution. It was hopeless: the British were masters of the field, and were interested in peace only after Isandlwana had been avenged. Not that the Zulus had lost the will to resist: on one occasion a young *ibutho* refused to allow Cetshwayo's peace emissaries to pass, and Chelmsford's advance was accomplished in the face of constant skirmishing. Among the casualties was the young Prince Imperial of France, exiled heir to the Bonapartist throne; in Zululand as an observer, he was out on patrol one day when ambushed by a Zulu scouting party.

At last, however, Chelmsford reached the vicinity of Ulundi and the complex of *amakhanda* on the Mahlabatini plain. Cetshwayo once more summoned his army, and the warriors dutifully mustered. The king and his *izinduna* made careful plans to attack the British. On the morning of 4 July Chelmsford crossed the White Mfolozi, and formed his troops up in a large rectangle opposite Ulundi. The *amabutho* appeared on the surrounding heights and advanced slowly to attack, greeted by the roll of volley fire, the boom of the guns, and the chatter of the Gatlings. For nearly an hour the Zulu commanders tried to direct their men against the British weak points; one charge, on the rear face of the rectangle, was sustained to within a few yards of the line. But the 'beast's horns' were of no use against an unbroken wall of defenders, and the Zulus faltered. Lord Chelmsford ordered the 17th Lancers to charge the broken enemy, and the Zulus were driven from the field.

The war was a calamity for the Zulus: battlefield casualties amounted to about 6,000 dead, and many more injured. Thousands of cattle were taken by the British, and not only the *amakhanda* but hundreds of civilian homesteads were destroyed.

King Dinuzulu kaCetshwayo, photographed at about the time of the rebellion in 1888. He wears European clothes, but also a variation of the 'bravery bead' necklace. (Author's collection)

The political, military, social and economic structure of the greater Zulu state was shattered. The king was a fugitive; on 28 August he was run to ground, captured by a British patrol, and began the long road to exile in Cape Town.

The army had gone to war in the traditional way, infused with the spirit of Shaka. True, many had not worn their ceremonial regalia; the evidence is patchy, but it seems that the majority of the main *impi* left behind the more complex and constricting items, and wore only loin coverings and perhaps a headband and a few cow tails—the younger *amabutho* seem to have worn very little. The *impi*

49

The Ruin of Zululand

A sketch by Baden-Powell—who fought against Dinuzulu in 1888—of a warrior wearing the *ubushokobezi* badge, the symbol of the uSuthu faction in the 1880s, later adopted by the rebels in 1906. (Author's collection)

The pacification and post-war settlement of Zululand was left to Lord Chelmsford's successor, Sir Garnet Wolseley. He tackled it with much vigour and little insight. The country was divided up into 13 small kingdoms. There was some attempt to dismantle the Zulu state—pre-Shakan clans were returned to prominence—and to exploit the divisions within the kingdom which had become apparent in 1879. Prince Hamu kaNzibe, who had defected to the British during the war—the only member of the royal house to do so—was given a kingdom, as was John Dunn, who had abandoned his protector Cetshwayo to serve as a scout for Chelmsford. Also honoured was Zibhebhu kaMaphita of the Mandhlakazi section. He was known to be a shrewd and ambitious leader, and favourable to the whites; he was no friend of Cetshwayo's, but had loyally fought in the war as an able commander. He was given a tract in northern Zululand which contained many of the clans most loyal to Cetshwayo.

Trouble started almost as soon as the British troops withdrew. Hamu, Zibhebhu and Dunn raided Cetshwayo's supporters—who called themselves the uSuthu, after the king's faction in 1856—in a deliberate attempt to destroy their authority. They retaliated, and appealed to Britain to restore the king.

Cetshwayo was imprisoned in reasonable comfort at Cape Town, where he petitioned to be allowed to return to his kingdom. The British had long since abandoned the Confederation scheme, and watched glumly as Zululand slid towards civil war. In September 1881 the king was allowed to visit London to state his case: he dined with Queen Victoria at Osborne House, and was a great success with the British public. The Foreign Office cautiously gave him permission to return home. In January 1883 he landed on the coast of Zululand.

He was given a small tract of land and no real power. Zibhebhu and Dunn were allowed to keep their lands and, though the king built a new homestead at Ulundi and formed new age-regiments, they were shorn of their military function and regalia and allowed to give ceremonial service only. It was made quite clear that no revival

which fought in the coastal region did not muster at Ulundi; it operated closer to the individual warriors' homes, and so seems to have retained more regalia in action. Yet the army remained committed to the old tactics of frontal assault, and did not exploit the full potential of its firepower; only towards the end of the campaign was there any reluctance to face the British in the open, and sniping increased. On at least two occasions—Isandlwana and Khambula—the young *amabutho* showed a serious lack of discipline by allowing themselves to be goaded into an attack against the wishes of their *izinduna*. This in turn reflected a lack of strong direction and control at the top. Wedded to an inappropriate tactical outlook which condemned them to waste their lives in open assault, the Zulus had taken to the field time and again, even when it became clear that there was no hope of victory. In the end, desperate courage was not enough: but the nation could ask no more of them.

of the old state system would be tolerated. The uSuthu leaders greeted him with delight, but Cetshwayo could neither succour them nor control them. He was powerless when the uSuthu in Zibhebhu's district rose up and attacked their tormenter. But Zibhebhu was too good a general for them; he abandoned his homestead to them and fell back to the Msebe valley, where he positioned his warriors in long grass in ambush. On 30 March they walked into the trap; the Mandhlakazi charged down on them, and in the subsequent rout as many as 4,000 uSuthu warriors were killed.

Cetshwayo watched in helpless misery as violence erupted across the country. The British blamed him for provoking it, but did nothing to stop it. Zibhebhu took matters into his own hands. On the morning of 21 July Cetshwayo awoke to find a Mandhlakazi *impi* bearing down on Ulundi. He still had *amabutho* at his disposal, but any weapons they carried were their own and they were hopelessly outclassed. The uSuthu were smashed and Zibhebhu sacked Ulundi, killing the *izinduna* he found there, the majority being *izikhulu* from the old days. Fifty-nine of them were killed in a slaughter which marked the real end of the old Zulu state.

The king himself was wounded in his flight from Ulundi, and took refuge in the remote Mhome Gorge, in the territory of Chief Sigananda of the

Chube clan in the rugged hill country above the Tugela. When he had recovered he went to the British magistracy at Eshowe, from where he tried to salvage something of the uSuthu fortunes. Here, on 8 February 1884, he died suddenly, officially of heart disease, though it was rumoured that he had been poisoned. His supporters took him back to the Chube territory, far away from the Mandhlakazi and British, and buried him.

Dinuzulu

His heir as leader of the luckless uSuthu and rightful king was his son Dinuzulu, who was not yet a teenager. Cetshwayo's full brother Prince Ndabuko kaMpande, and Chief Mnyamana of the Buthelezi clan, formerly head of Cetshwayo's *ibandla*, acted as regents. They turned to the British for help, and when that was not forthcoming accepted an offer from the Transvaal Boers, who promised military support against the Mandhlakazi. On 21 May 1884 the Boers proclaimed Dinuzulu king—a title the British refused to acknowledge—and then set out to attack Zibhebhu. They caught up with him on 5 June in a natural amphitheatre formed between the Gaza and Etshaneni mountains. As at Msebe, Zibhebhu prepared an elaborate ambush, but the

Redcoats in Zululand, 1883: the garrison of Fort Northampton, on the Zulu bank at Rorke's Drift. (Brian Maggs)

trap sprung prematurely, and his warriors had to move into the open to attack. The Boers, firing from the saddle over the heads of the attacking uSuthu, cut the Mandhlakazi warriors down. Zibhebhu fled to Natal, and the Boers presented the bill: they claimed farms from Dinuzulu stretched across most of Zululand.

This was not what the uSuthu leaders had had in mind, and once more they appealed to Britain. This time the British listened, if only because the prospect of a Boer route to the sea, which would open communication with Germany, was held to be a direct challenge to British strategic interests in southern Africa. Negotiations with the Boers forced

Chief Bhambatha kaMancinza of the Zondi clan, the leader of the 1906 rebellion. (Africana Museum, Johannesburg)

them to restrict their claims, and on 9 May 1887 Zululand was finally annexed by Britain.

The annexation brought Zululand under the control of Natal's Native Law, and magistracies were established across the country. Dinuzulu, however, free of the Mandhlakazi challenge, set about restoring his authority. When he tried to have a man executed for witchcraft the magistrate summoned him to explain himself. He refused to attend and was promptly fined, and told that Zibhebhu would be allowed to return to his old lands. This was intended as a check to balance Dinuzulu's power, but it provoked a violent explosion. When Zibhebhu and a number of his adherents turned up to claim their old lands they found the uSuthu in possession. The local magistrate used his small force of native police (the *Nongqayi*) to evict the uSuthu; but in March 1888 an uSuthu chief refused to vacate his homestead, and called out his warriors. Dinuzulu was blamed for inciting rebellion, but when a party of soldiers went to arrest him they found him entrenched in a rocky outcrop known as Ceza Mountain, accompanied by 1,800 armed warriors recruited from the loyal uSuthu clans. A sharp fight ensued, and the troops had to withdraw leaving two dead on the field. All over the country the jubilant uSuthu rose up, raiding the homesteads of their enemies.

The magistracy at Nongoma in the centre of the country was seriously threatened. A refuge for white traders and farmers, it was defended by a small party of *Nongqayi*. Orders were sent to Zibhebhu asking him to reinforce the post, and he arrived with about 800 warriors and camped on a nearby hill. On the morning of 23 June about 4,000 uSuthu, led by Dinuzulu himself, attacked the post. The uSuthu *impi* divided in two, one portion attacking the magistracy, the greater portion falling on the Mandhlakazi. The Nongqayi drove their attackers off, but the uSuthu onslaught broke the Mandhlakazi, and once more Zibhebhu fled. It was to be his last military campaign—he lived quietly near Eshowe for a while before returning to his hereditary lands, where he died in 1905.

The attack on Nongoma was the uSuthu high-water mark. The British collected together a larger force, and on 2 July defeated the uSuthu at Hlopekulu Mountain, near Ulundi. Dinuzulu, Ndabuko and Prince Shingana kaMpande attempted to flee to the Transvaal, but they were turned away and went instead to Natal, where they surrendered. They were tried for treason and sentenced to exile on St. Helena.

The 1888 rebellion proved to be the last time the Zulu royal house went to war—a ghost of 1879, with Zulus once more meeting British soldiers in the field. There was to be one last tragic uprising; but, though the rebels tried to draw on the prestige of the old military system and the Zulu kings, its causes and supporters lay, for the most part, outside the traditions of the old Zulu state.

Rebel dead on the battlefield, July 1906. The amount of European clothing suggests that they are Natal rebels. Note the small size of the shield, typical of this period. (Africana Museum, Johannesburg)

Bhambatha

With the exile of Dinuzulu, Zululand became peaceful at last. In 1897 Britain handed it over to the Colony of Natal, and areas were opened up for European settlement. Dinuzulu was allowed to return to his old homestead, though the Government recognised him as a chief and not a king. Despite the heavy fighting in Natal the Boer War did not affect Zululand much—although one Boer commando angered the abaQulusi, as aggressive as ever, and was attacked one night at Holkranz, losing 56 of 59 of their number.

Nevertheless, the 1890s were not kind to the African population of Natal and Zululand. The

The entrance to Mhome Gorge, the site of the decisive battle of the 1906 rebellion. The rebel overnight camp was where the homestead now stands, at centre right. The Colonial forces ringed the surrounding heights. (Author's collection)

land reserved for them was cramped, and over-grazing brought about soil erosion. Cattle herds were decimated by rinderpest, and locusts ate their crops. When the Natal authorities, seeking to balance their budget in the post-Boer War recession, imposed a poll tax, it was the last straw. Many chiefs refused to pay; others sent to Dinuzulu, whom they still regarded as their king, for advice. He advised them to pay. Still some would not, and parties of police sent to collect the tax were driven off.

The country seemed to be ripe for rebellion; and a leader emerged in Bhambatha kaMancinza of the Zondi clan, who lived in the spectacular Mpanza valley on the Natal side of the Tugela. Bhambatha was in his mid-forties, a chief of no great rank, who had a reputation for faction fights. When he refused to pay the tax and police were sent to arrest him, he slipped across the border to consult Dinuzulu.

Privately Dinuzulu may have sympathised with Bhambatha, but he would not countenance rebellion: he did, however, allow Bhambatha to leave his family at his homestead. Buoyed up by what he took as tacit approval, Bhambatha returned to Natal, gathered his fighting men and, on the night of 4 April 1906 attacked a police patrol. In a stiff fight four whites were killed, and the body of one was used by Bhambatha's war-doctor to make medicine. He and his warriors then crossed into Zululand and made for the territory of Chief Sigananda of the Chube. Sigananda was in his nineties, and had served under Shaka as an *udibi*. He was steadfastly loyal to the Zulu royal house, and asked Dinuzulu whether he should join the rebels. Dinuzulu was evasive and Sigananda threw in his lot with Bhambatha.

In Natal, meanwhile, a state of emergency had been declared, and the militia called out. A force was put together under the command of Col. (later Sir) Duncan McKenzie, and marched out from Eshowe into the jumble of steep ridges and bush-choked valleys which comprised the Chube district.

The rebels had made the grave of King Cetshwayo their rallying point, and towards this the Colonial forces advanced. On 5 May they were descending a steep ridge known as Bope, when about 1,000 rebels burst from the bush and charged on them. The rebels were wearing a distinctive badge known as the *uboshokobezi*, a stiff piece of white cowhide or cow tail worn upright on the headdress; this was a deliberate identification with the Zulu kings, as the uSuthu had adopted this badge in the 1880s. Several had guns, but most carried spears and small shields which they held up before their faces as they ran—Bhambatha's doctors had told him that the white man's bullets would turn to water. They did not: and the rebels were driven off with heavy losses.

Mhome Gorge

The fight at Bope ushered in several weeks of sweeps and skirmishes. Bhambatha at least, had learnt something from the past: his men did not try the massed assaults of old, but tried to lure the whites on to disadvantageous ground to ambush them. Several times they gave McKenzie a run for his money. Then, on the night of 9–10 June 1906, McKenzie received an intelligence report that several rebel *impis*—including Bhambatha's—had converged on Sigananda's stronghold, the Mhome Gorge, and were camped at the entrance. McKenzie issued orders for his own scattered forces to advance upon the gorge.

The gorge itself is narrow and steep, the sides falling almost sheer for 1,000 feet in places. At the far end was a waterfall, a spot so inaccessible that Cetshwayo had hidden there after his defeat by Zibhebhu. The rebels believed that once they had entered the gorge they would be impregnable. This had made them careless: they spent the night at the

Chief Sigananda of the Chube (with bandaged ankles) photographed with Col. McKenzie (second from right) after his surrender. The old chief had been an *udibi* servant in Shaka's army, and was the most important Zulu leader to support Bhambatha in 1906; his career thus spanned the rise and fall of the Zulu nation. (Killie Campbell Library)

report spoke of 600 rebel dead, but the real total was much higher. Among them was Bhambatha. He had been killed in a mêlée with Natal levies in the bottom of the gorge, but it was several days before he was recognised. It was imperative that proof of his death be made known; since it was impossible to recover his body, his head was cut off and taken to Natal for identification.

The battle at Mhome Gorge ended the rebellion in Zululand. Sigananda surrendered, and died later in prison. There was to be a further uprising in June across the Tugela in the Natal district of Mapumulo. Several battles occurred in the rugged country around the trading station of Thring's Post, but in the end machine guns prevailed over assegais. Nearly 5,000 rebels were brought to trial, the ringleaders exiled and the rest imprisoned. Among them was Dinuzulu kaMpande, who many believed was behind the uprising. That he had sheltered Bhambatha's wife told against him; he was convicted and sentenced to four years' imprisonment. He was not allowed to return to Zululand, and died in 1913 in the Transvaal, the last of the Zulu warrior kings. His followers took his body back to Zululand, and buried him in the heart of Zulu country, not far from where Shaka had begun his conquests.

*　　*　　*

Today there are over six million Zulus in South Africa, and they acknowledge Dinuzulu's great-grandson, Goodwill Zwelithini, as their hereditary king. Their principal political leader, Chief Mangosutho Buthelezi, is internationally renowned, and the memories of the warrior past are a significant source of national pride. Archaeologists have reconstructed part of King Cetshwayo's Ulundi homestead: it stands opposite the Legislative Assembly of modern KwaZulu on Mahlabatini plain.

The Plates

A: The youth of Shaka

A1: Nandi bids farewell to her son as he sets off to join the Mthethwa army in about 1805. The dress of a married woman at that time was very simple: the characteristic top-knot coloured with red ochre,

A detail from a famous study by Angas of a warrior of the *amaShishi* (*isaNqu*) regiment in the 1840s, showing the construction of the headdress. This man is not wearing a headband, so the shape of the *amaphovela*, and the way the 'earflaps' of this example fall down each side of the back of the head, are clearly shown. Note how the *isakabuli* feathers are tied to quills and thrust into the sides of the headdress. (Author's collection)

entrance and their sentries failed to notice McKenzie's approach. This had been a remarkable feat in itself, co-ordinating an advance over such impossible ground in the dark; but as dawn broke the rebels found themselves surrounded by troops on all the overlooking heights. The rebels' strength was estimated at about 20 *amaviyo*, or companies—perhaps 1,500 men. The Colonial force included 15pdr. artillery and Colt machine-guns.

As soon as the rebels realised their predicament, they formed a circle to receive instructions; seeing this, the Colonial troops opened fire. It was a massacre. Shot and shell rained down on the rebels from all sides. They broke, and fled back into the gorge. This proved to be no more than a trap, and for several hours the troops shot them down at leisure. At last they descended from the heights and swept the bush, flushing out survivors. The official and a leather skirt. Nandi was renowned for her beauty and her fiery temperament, and so would probably have liked to wear beads (then scarce, and something of a luxury) and brass bangles.

A2: Shaka. This reconstruction is largely speculative; he is shown wearing the typical dress of a young warrior of the period—a leopardskin headband and sakabuli feathers. The cords around the body were made of twisted strips of lambskin, and were worn on festive occasions. At this stage the war shields were small and probably not uniform in colour. Sandals would have been worn.

A3: Mthethwa chief. He wears a leopardskin collar, to which only men of rank were entitled; the necklace of leopard claws and the bunch of lourie feathers in the headdress are also marks of distinction. He has a typical snuff-spoon tucked into his *isicoco* (headring) and carries a wooden staff, which also seems to have

been a symbol of chief's rank. All of these items were essentially 'civilian' in their significance, but were often carried over into the military sphere.

B/C: The Battle of Gqokli Hill, 1818
B/C 1: Warrior of the Isipezi ibutho or age group regiment. There is very little direct evidence relating to the uniforms of Shaka's regiments, so these tentative reconstructions are necessarily based on comparisons of fragmentary Zulu and European sources. The Isipezi seem to have carried white shields patterned across the middle with black spots, and to have worn crane feathers in their headdress.

B/C 2: Ndwandwe commander, based on a description by a British naval officer who encountered a party

A modern reconstruction—ignore the metal buckles—of a pair of cow tail leg ornaments, basically similar in appearance to the 19th-century originals. (Africana Museum, Johannesburg)

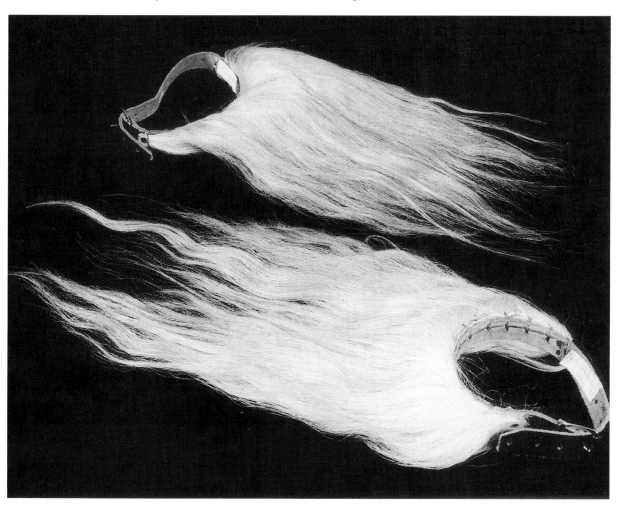

A modern reconstruction of the *umqhele* or leopardskin headband; the earflaps—*amabheqe*—appear considerably larger in early sketches and photographs. (Africana Museum, Johannesburg)

of Ndwandwe wandering north after their defeat by Shaka in 1819. He wears a single crane feather in his headdress, and a kilt of civet and samango tails around his waist and body. Like the Zulus, the Ndwandwe would also have used cow tails as part of their war dress. At the time of Gqokli Hill the Ndwandwe would have been carrying small shields and throwing-spears, and wearing sandals.

B/C 3: King Shaka kaSenzangakhona. We have a detailed description of Shaka's war dress from *The Diary of Henry Francis Fynn*, one of the British traders who visited his court. He wore a collar and kilt of twisted tails, cow tails around his arms and legs, and a headdress with bunches of lourie feathers and one crane feather. His shield was white with one black spot.

B/C 4: Warrior of the Fasimba, Shaka's favourite regiment, who carried white shields and probably wore sakabuli feathers in the headdress. This man wears the marks of distinction of a brave veteran: a bunch of lourie feathers in the headdress, a brass *ingxotha* armband, and bravery beads around the

body. There is evidence to suggest that in this early period strips of civet or monkey skin were sewn into old spear-slits in the shield to draw attention to the warrior's prowess.

B/C 5: Young Ndwandwe warrior. There is even less information on the Ndwandwe than on the Zulus of this period; but a number of Zulu-style features remained in the dress of the Ndwandwe splinter groups—the Ngoni and Shangane—which presumably originated in Zululand, and which confirm what one would expect: that Ndwandwe and Zulu dress were similar. This warrior wears a headdress of sakabuli feathers, typical of a young man's costume.

A bunch of *isakabuli* feathers, as worn by young warriors, here mounted on a base for wearing on top of the head. Note too the *umqhele* at bottom right, here of cheetah fur. (Natal Museum, Pietermaritzburg)

B/C 6: Warrior of the Ndabezibona, a section of the Fasimba, who carried black shields with a white spot in the centre. The full dress of the Fasimba is not known, but would have included all the elements usual for a young *ibutho*. This man has a porcupine quill in his headband, which was not purely decorative—it was used for removing thorns from the feet.

B/C 7: Senior Ndwandwe warrior, wearing a single ostrich feather in his headdress. The names of several of Chief Zwide's *amabutho* survive, suggesting that his army was well organised, albeit not to the Zulu standard. This may well have been a regimental uniform, although it seems unlikely that the shield colour was consistent or significant.

D: The first meeting between Europeans and King Shaka, 1824

D1: Lt. Francis Farewell had served in the Royal Navy until the end of the Napoleonic Wars. He wore at least part of his uniform on his first meeting with the king, and we show him here with an 1815 lieutenant's coat. Since he rode part of the way to Bulawayo, we have shown him in civilian riding breeches and boots.

D2: Imbongi, or praise-singer (pl. *izimbongi*). A feature of the Zulu court, such men wore fantastic costumes of their own devising, and danced and capered before the king calling out the praise-poems which recalled his heroic deeds. This man is shown wearing items recorded as typical of an *imbongi*—long braided hair coloured with ochre, a headring, antelope horns as a headdress, and cow tails and leopardskin around the body.

D3: King Shaka. There is some dispute as to whether Shaka was married; however, there are a number of references to his barber trimming his hair around his *isicoco*, so we have shown him wearing the headring. He would, of course, have worn different costumes for different occasions, but this seems to have been his most frequent 'official' dress. At this time the king was about 38 years old.

D4: Shaka's interpreter. A Xhosa from the eastern Cape frontier, captured by the British in one of the many 'Kaffir' Wars, he accompanied one of the exploratory missions to Natal, where he escaped and made his way to kwaBulawayo. The king was quick to appreciate the value of his talents. His Xhosa name was Msimbiti, but the whites called him Jacob or Jakot, and the Zulus, Hlambamanzi—'the swimmer'—since he had swum ashore from a boat to escape. He wears a blanket in the Xhosa fashion.

E: The court of Dingane, 1830s
E1: Youth in dancing dress. Dancing was a very important social activity, both as part of national festivals and simply for pleasure. Kings Dingane and Mpande were particularly fond of organising and taking part in dances in which hundreds or even thousands participated. This youth in festive dress is based on a sketch by George French Angas; the coloured fringes are of beadwork.

E2: King Dingane in dancing dress, based on sketches from life by the missionary Capt. Allen Gardiner. Dingane took a great personal interest in his own dancing costume and that of his female attendants, and liked to experiment with different combinations of beads, bangles and feathers. His chair, carved from a single block of wood, still exists. His shield was black with one white spot.

E3: Ndlela kaSompisi, Dingane's chief *induna* and most talented general, carries his war shield and wears the full kilt. The brass rings would have been given to him by the king, who distributed them to his favourites. In battle he would probably have

A pair of *izingxotha*, the brass armbands distributed by Zulu kings to warriors who had shown particular daring in battle; the exact design varied slightly over the years—these date from Cetshwayo's reign. (RRW Museum, Brecon)

worn an otter-skin headband, a crane feather, and perhaps lourie feathers.

F: Skirmish between Boers and Zulus, December 1838
F1: Boer Voortrekker ('those who trek to the fore'). The Boers fought in their everyday clothes, which at this time included short jackets or waistcoats, wide-brimmed hats and *veldschoen*—light home-made shoes of hide. Their weapons were flintlock or percussion muskets; ammunition was carried in leather bags slung over the shoulder, though powderhorns were sometimes attached to the waistbelt.

F2: Warrior, probably of the Mbelebele, Dingane's favourite regiment, based on a sketch by Gardiner. There is surprisingly little information on Dingane's *amabutho*. Gardiner's original sketch describes the warrior as 'partly panoplied', presumably meaning war dress. The cow tail necklace is a lighter variant of the full-dress type. The Mbelebele were quartered at King Dingane's personal residence, emGungundhlovu.

F3: Warrior of the Kokoti regiment in war dress. The Kokoti were ordered by the king to carry only knobkerries, and these were apparently slung—bizarrely enough—down the back, from a neck thong. This unusual dictate was reportedly a punishment for the regiment having mocked other *amabutho* for having failed to defeat the Boers and boasting that they could do so even without spears.

G: The Battle of 'Ndondakasuka, December 1856
G1: Warrior of the uDhloko regiment. This *ibutho* apparently wore most of their ceremonial regalia into action at this battle, where they formed part of the uSuthu forces. At this date they were unmarried, and wore a spectacular headdress of black and white ostrich feathers intermixed. The same regiment later took part in the Zulu War of 1879, wearing a costume modified to reflect their more senior status. Note the smaller *umbhumbuluzo* shield.

G2: Prince Cetshwayo kaMpande, in the costume he wore at this battle; he took an active part in the engagement, leading the centre of the uSuthu forces. He is wearing an *umutsha* of black lambskin, and an *ibeshu* of samango monkey skin. He carries the shield of the Thulwana regiment—at this date unmarried—and wears a single crane feather reflecting his royal status, despite his lack of the headring. He is also wearing a necklace of magical charms, and carrying a civilian percussion shotgun.

G3: Warrior of the Impisi regiment, which formed part of Prince Mbuyazi's iziGqoza faction. The iziGqoza apparently adopted a headdress similar to the *amaphovela* as its badge.

H: Warriors on their way to muster, 1870s
H1: Zulu girls. Unmarried girls were also organised into age group guilds, but they were not required to live barracked together like the youths. They had no military function, but particular age groups would be allocated to male regiments, and the warriors would choose their brides from among them. Basic dress consisted of nothing more than a short skirt, though beads were extremely popular as ornamentation.

A particularly fine example of a charm necklace, consisting of snake- and animal-skin pouches of magical medicine, teeth, and various selected blocks of wood, some of them ritually burnt at the edges. This example was acquired from one of Cetshwayo's war doctors by Lt.Col. A. W. Durnford, who was later killed at Isandlwana. (Royal Engineers Museum)

H2: Warrior of the Mtuyisazwe, a regiment incorporated into the outsize corps named uKhandempemvu or umCijo. The Mtuyisazwe wore *amaphovela* headdress, and carried black shields with a white spot across the centre; they also wore a wide cowhide waist belt.

H3: Warrior of the uKhandempemvu; his costume is quite distinct from that of H2, even though they were considered to be part of the same unit. He wears a bunch of sakabuli feathers on top of his head, and carries a red shield; other companies of the same regiment carried black shields. Both H2 and H3 are of the same age group. The uKhandempemvu played a significant part in the battle of Isandlwana; the full regalia shown here would not, however, have been worn in action.

H4: Udibi boy. These were boys of pre-cadet age who acted as servants for individual warriors, carrying their food or, as here, sleeping mats and other possessions.

I: The court of Mpande, 1870s
I1: King Mpande kaSenzangakhona dancing with his warriors at an *umkhosi* ceremony, c.1870. Although obese, the king was said to have been a graceful

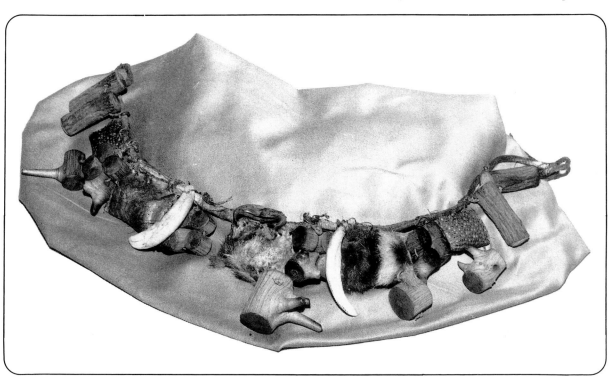

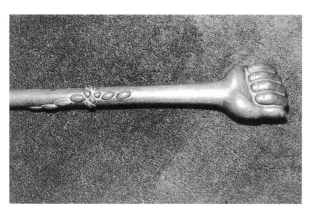

The beautifully carved head of King Cetshwayo's staff. (S. Bourquin)

dancer even at the end of his life. His festive costume was extremely lavish: his body was covered with monkey skin and cow tails, and his headdress consisted of black ostrich feathers, large bunches of lourie feathers, and a crane feather. His shield was white with a small mark, and he carried a black-wood dancing stick.

I2: Warrior of the umXapho regiment. In the 1870s differences between full ceremonial uniforms were slight. The umXapho wore ostrich feathers all over their heads, and carried black shields.

I3: Warrior of the iNdlu-yengwe regiment; note the similarity with the costume of I2. The differences lie mainly in the arrangement of the ostrich feathers, and the fact that the iNdlu-yengwe have sakabuli feathers. They also have white spots low down on their shields. On festive occasions the warriors would not have carried spears.

J: An impi being doctored for war, 1870s
J1: Isangoma. Braided hair and a plethora of magical charms distinguish the dress of the diviner; he also wears rattles made from insect cocoons around his ankles. As part of the ceremony the *isangoma* cut strips of meat from a slaughtered bull, treated them with magical potions, and threw them to the warriors, who were each expected to take a bite.

J2: Warrior of the iNgobamakhosi regiment in full dress. He wears an *amaphovela* headdress with feathers of the black-tailed finch (*isakabuli*); and an *ingxotha* armlet of the type favoured by King Cetshwayo on

his right arm. His shield is red and white, although other companies of the regiment almost certainly carried black, or black and white shields. The iNgobamakhosi was a very large regiment, and a favourite of the king's.

J3: Warrior of the Thulwana regiment. Compare with Plate G2. The Thulwana had many men of high status within their ranks, and their uniform was correspondingly lavish. They wore the full kilt, and several brass bands on the right arm. Their shields—here an *isihlangu*, but both types were carried—were white with small red or black marks. Both the iNgobamakhosi and the Thulwana were members of the Undi corps—quartered at Ulundi—but there was a fierce rivalry between them, and they could not in fact live together. Both regiments played a prominent part in the fighting of 1879.

K: The aftermath of Isandlwana, 22 January 1879
K1: Warrior of the Mbonambi regiment. He moves with his comrades through the wreckage of the camp at Isandlwana, looting, stripping and disembowelling the enemy dead in accordance with custom. This regiment seems to have been formed and re-formed several times, but in 1879 it comprised unmarried men in their early thirties. There are conflicting descriptions of the headdress, but little of this was worn into action beyond, perhaps, a headband and bunch of lourie feathers. This man has a charm necklace, which were very popular at this time. It seems to have been up to individuals how much of their costume they retained on campaign.

K2: Warrior of the iNdlondlo regiment, a 900-strong unit incorporated into the Thulwana. The full dress uniform was similar to that of the Thulwana, but nothing so lavish would have been worn into action.

K3: Warrior of the iNgobamakhosi regiment. The young regiments in 1879 seem to have worn very little regalia into action: perhaps the *umqhele*, a charm necklace, and sometimes cow tails around the arms and legs, but little else apart from the loin covering. He has put on the tunic of a soldier of the 24th Regiment whom he killed, in accordance with ritual. Large numbers of breach-loading rifles fell into Zulu hands after the battle.

L: The Battle of Mhome Gorge, 10 June 1906

L1: Zulu rebel, wearing the *ubushokobezi* badge and cast-off European clothing, and carrying a small shield typical of the period. Eyewitness accounts mention that some rebels still wore the working overalls of the Castle brewery.

L2: Private, Durban Light Infantry, the principal Colonial infantry unit to see action in the 1906 rebellion. The DLI wore khaki tropical field service uniforms similar to those of the British regulars in the Boer War, although the sun helmet was of a slightly different shape. Equipment was of the Slade-Wallace pattern.

L3: Constable of the Nongqayi, the Zululand Native Police. The Nongqayi were raised in the 1880s; despite the distinguished service they rendered during the 1888 uprising they were disbanded shortly afterwards in deference to the fears of many Colonists about arming Africans. They were, however, re-formed at the outbreak of Bhambatha's rebellion in 1906, and proved tenacious fighters. Their uniform consisted of a blue jacket with breast pockets, and blue trousers cut off below the knee. They carried Martini-Henry rifles and had black Slade-Wallace equipment. At Mhome Gorge they seem to have worn blue jerseys.

The present king of the Zulus, HM King Goodwill Zwelithini kaCyprian, dressed in ceremonial regalia which has changed only slightly since King Shaka's day. (Author's collection)

Notes sur les planches en couleur

A1 La mère de Shaka dit au-revoir à son fils, vers 1805. Elle porte la robe simple des femmes mariées: coiffure de noeuds de rubans teints à l'ocre, jupe de cuir, perles et bracelets. **A2** Shaka porte le costume typique des jeunes guerriers—sandales, bandeau en peau de léopard orné de plumes de *sakabuli*. **A3** Les chefs de tribu se distinguaient, par exemple, par un collier de griffes de léopard et un bâton en bois indiquant leur rang. Ce chef porte également une cuillère à tabac dans son serre-tête.

B/C1 Guerrier portant le bouclier du régiment des Isipezi—blanc orné de taches noires en son centre. **B/C2** D'après la description faite par un officier de marine britannique, ce commandant Ndwandwe porte une plume de grue unique dans sa coiffure et un kilt de queues de civette et de singe. **B/C3** Le Roi Shaka à la bataille de la Colline de Gqokli, 1818. **B/C4** Le régiment des Fasimba, qui était équipé d'un bouclier blanc, était le préféré de Shaka. Ce guerrier porte un bouquet de plumes de lourie dans son bandeau, un brassard *ingxotha* en cuivre, et des perles sur tout le corps en signe de bravoure. **B/C5** Jeune guerrier de la tribu des Ndwandwe. Comme les zoulous, le Ndwandwe portaient des plumes de sakabuli dans leur serre-tête. **B/C6** Ce guerrier Ndabezibone porte le bouclier du régiment des Fasimba. Le piquant de porc-épi qu'il porte dans son bandeau lui était utile pour se retirer les épines des pieds. **B/C7** Guerrier Ndwandwe de rang supérieur, reconnaissable à l'unique plume d'autruche qu'il porte dans sa coiffure.

D1 Le Lieutenant Francis Farewell fut le premier Européen à rencontrer Shaka. En 1824 il se rendit à cheval de Port Natal à Bulawayo et Shaka fit de son mieux pour l'impressionner par la puissance et la richesse de son royaume. **D2** Les *imbongi* ou 'chanteurs de louanges' avaient pour rôle de danser devant le roi en récitant ses exploits héroïques. Cet *imbongi* porte le costume extravagant typique qui comprenait de longues nattes, des cornes d'antilope en guise de coiffure, et des queues de vache et une peau de léopard autour du corps. **D3** Le roi Shaka, âgé

Farbtafeln

A1 Shakas mutter sagt Lebewohl zu ihrem Sohn (ca.1805). Sie wird in der einfachen Kleidung einer verheirateten Frau gezeigt: ihr Haarknoten ist ockerfarben, sie trägt einen Lederrock sowie Holzperlenketten und Armreifen. **A2** Shaka trägt die typische Tracht eines jungen Kriegers—Sandalen, ein Stirnband aus Leopardenfell und *Sakabuli*-Federn. **A3** Der Stammeshäuptling unterschied sich z. B. durch Halsketten aus Leopardenkrallen und hölzerne Amtsstäbe. Ausserdem hat er einen Schnupftabaklöffel im Kopfring befestigt.

B/C1 Ein Krieger trägt das weisse Schild mit schwarzen Punkten über der Mitte; er gehört zum Isipezi Regiment. **B/C2** Ein britischer Marineoffizier beschrieb diesen Ndwandwe Führer, dessen Kopfbedeckung eine einzige Kranichfeder zierte und der in einem Rock aus Zibetkatzen—und Affenschwänzen gekleidet war. **B/C3** König Shaka während der Schlacht von Gqokli Hill (1818). **B/C4** Shakas Lieblingsregiment, das weisse Schilder trug, war das Fasimba. Das Stirnband dieses Kriegers ist mit einem Lourie Federstutz geschmückt, darüber hinaus trägt er einen aus Messing gefertigten *ingxotha* Armreif und Glas/holzperlenketten, um seinen Körper als Zeichen seiner Tapferkeit. **B/C5** Ein junger Krieger des Stammes der Ndwandwe. Wie die Zulu, trugen auch die Ndwandwe *Sakabuli*-Federn im Stirnreif. **B/C6** Dieser Ndabezibone Krieger ist mit dem Schild des Fasimba Regiments ausgerüstet. Die Stachel, die von eimen Stachelschwein stammten und im Stirnband angebracht waren, wurden auch zum Entfernen von Dornen aus der Fusssohle benutzt. **B/C7** Der ranghöchste Ndwandwe Krieger zeichnete sich durch eine einzige Straussenfeder in seiner Kopfbedeckung aus.

D1 Lieutenant Francis Farewell war der erste Europäer den Shaka zu Gesicht bekam. Im Jahre 1824 ritt er von Port Natal nach Bulawayo und Shaka unternahm sein tunlichstes, ihn mit dem Einfluss und dem Reichtum seines Königreichs zu beeindrucken. **B2** Die *Imbongi* oder 'Lobsänger' tanzten vor dem König und erzählten von seinen Heldentaten. Seine phantasievolle Tracht setzte d'environ 38 ans, porte son costume 'officiel' ordinaire. **D4** L'interprète de Shaka porte une couverture à la façon de la tribu Xhosa à laquelle il appartenait.

E1 La danse était une activité sociale importante à la cour du roi Dingane entre 1830 et 1840; ce jeune homme porte le costume typique des danseurs. **E2** D'après des croquis effectués par un missionnaire, le Capitaine Allen Gardiner, le roi Dingane porte une couverture à la façon des danseurs. Ndela kaSompisi, conseiller en chef de Dingane et général de grand talent portant son bouclier de guerre et son kilt. Le roi lui avait sans doute donné les anneaux de cuivre.

F1 Boer Vortrekker, 1838. Les Boers allaient au combat en vêtements ordinaires et utilisaient des fusils à pierres ou des mousquets à percussion. **F2** Costume de combat des Mbelebele, régiment préféré de Dingane. **F3** Les membres du régiment des Kokoti avaient reçu l'ordre de ne se battre qu'avec une massue grossière, qu'ils portaient pendue dans le dos à l'aide d'une courroie passée autour du cou; ils avaient été ainsi punis pour leur vantardise.

G1 Les membres du régiment des uDhloko portaient la plupart de leurs insignes d'apparat au combat, ainsi ce guerrier célibataire porte une coiffure spectaculaire faite de plumes d'autruche noires et blanches. Remarquez le petit bouclier *umbhumbuluzo*. **G2** Le prince Cetshwayo kaMpande à la bataille de 'Ndondakasuka', 1856; il porte une plume de grue unique qui indique son rang royal et un collier d'amulettes magiques. **G3** Le régiment des Impisi adoptèrent une coiffure similaire à celle des *amaphovela* comme emblème du regiment.

H1 Les jeunes filles célibataires étaient elles aussi organisées en corps selon leur âge, bien que ceux-ci naient pas eu de rôle militaire. Le costume de base consistait en une jupe courte et des perles. **H2** Guerrier du régiment des Mtuyisazwe portant un bouclier noir à tache blanche et une ceinture de peau de vache. **H3** L'uniforme de ce guerrier du régiment des uKhandempemvu est assez distinct de celui de H2; il porte un bouclier rouge et un bouquet de plumes de *sakabuli* sur la tête. **H4** Jeune garçon *udibi*; les jeunes *udibi* étaient employés comme serviteurs personnels par les guerriers.

I1 Le roi Mpande kaSenzangakhoma dansant avec ses guerriers, vers 1870. Le costume de fête du roi consistait en une peau de singe et des queues de vache, et sa coiffure de plumes d'autruche blanches, de plumes de lourie et d'une plume de grue. **I2** Entre les années 1870 et 1880 les différences entre les uniformes des différents régiments s'étaient presqu'effacées. Ce guerrier umXapho porte des plumes d'autruche tout autour de la tête et un bouclier noir. **I3** Le régiment des iNdlu-yengwe portait un costume très semblable à celui de I2: la différence principale est la disposition des plumes et les taches blanches placées bas sur le bouclier.

J1 Le *isangoma* ou 'devin' jouait un rôle important dans les préparatifs des armées au combat. Il se distinguait par ses tresses et les amulettes magiques pendues sur tout son corps. **J2** Guerrier du régiment des iNgobamakhosi en costume. Il porte une coiffure à cornes et un bouclier rouge et blanc. **J3** Le régiment des Thulwana étaient en rivalité avec celui des iNgobamakhosi et bien qu'ils aient été tous les deux logés a Ulundi, ils se battaient trop pour pouvoir vivre en paix ensemble.

K1 Ce guerrier du régiment des Mbonambi s'apprête à effectuer les mutilations rituelles qui étaient pratiquées sur les ennemis morts après la bataille. **K2** L'uniforme complet du régiment des iNdlondlo était beaucoup trop somptueux pour être porté au combat, de sorte que ce guerrier porte très peu d'insignes d'apparat. **K3** Comme K2 ce guerrier iNgobamakhosi porte très peu d'insignes, mais il a récupéré la tunique d'un soldat du 24ème Régiment. Un grand nombre de fusils se chargeant par la culasse tombèrent aux mains des Zoulous après la bataille de Isandlwana.

L1 Ce rebelle zoulou à la bataille des Gorges de Mhome porte des vêtements de rebut européens et l'emblème du *ubushokobezi* sur sa coiffure. **L2** Les soldats de l'Infanterie Légère de Durban portaient des uniformes de service tropicaux khaki semblables à ceux des troupes régulières britanniques, à part le casque colonial qui était de forme légèrement différente. **L3** Ce policier appartenait aux Nongqayi, Forces de Police Indigènes du Zoulouland, porte un fusil *Martini-Henry* et un équipement *Slade-Wallace* noir.

sich aus geflochtenem Haar, einem Antilopengeweih als Kopfschmuck, sowie aus Kuh—und Leopardenschwänzen am Körper, zusammen. **D3** König Shaka im Alter von *ca.* 38 Jahren, ist in seiner üblichen 'Amtstracht' zu sehen. **D4** Shakas Dolmetscher hat eine Decke, in der Art wie sie der Stamm der Xhosa trägt, um seinen Körper geschlungen.

E1 In den dreissiger Jahren des vorigen Jahrhunderts, war der Tanz eine bedeutende Form der Unterhaltung am Hofe des König Dingane; dieser junge Mann trägt die typische Tanzkleidung. **E2** Auf Skizzen des Missionärs Capt. Allen Gardiner beruhend wurde König Dingane in der Tanzkleidung, gekleidet mit Holsperlenketten, Armreifen und Federn, dargestellt. **E3** Ndlela kaSompisi, Dinganes ranghöchster Berater und geschickter General trägt sein Kriegsschild und den vollen Rock. Die Messingringe wurden ihm wohl vom König überreicht.

F1 Boer Voortrekker im Jahre 1838. Die Buren kämpften in ihrer gewöhnlichen Kleidung und benutzen Steinschloss—und Perkussions-Gewehre. **F2** Kriegsbekleidung der Mbelebele—Dinganes Lieblingsregiment. **F3** Dem Kokoti Regiment wurde befohlen nur mit Knüppel mit Knauf in den Kampf zu ziehen, welche sie über den Rücken geschlungen und am Halsriemen befestigt trugen. Dies galt als Bestrafung für Prahlerei.

G1 Das uDhloko Regiment trug den grössten Teil der zeremoniellen Tracht im Kampf. Dieser ledige Krieger trägt einen atemberaubenden Kopfschmuck aus schwarzen und weissen Straussenfedern. Auffällig ist auch das kleinere *umbhumbuluzo* Schild. **G2** Prinz Cetshwayo kaMpande während der Schlacht von 'Ndondaksuka im Jahre 1856. Die einzelne Kranichfeder deutet auf seinen königlichen Rang, überdies trägt er eine Halskette mit Talisman-Anhängern. **G3** Das Impisi Regiment übernahm eine ähnliche Kopfbedeckung, die dem Abzeichen der *amaphovela* entsprach.

H1 Unverheiratete Mädchen wurden gemäss ihrer Altersgruppen in Gilden zusammengefasst, obgleich ihnen keine militärische Funktion zugeordnet wurde. Ihre Tracht bestand aus einem kurzen Rock und Glas/Holzperlenketten. **H2** Krieger des Mtuyisazwe Regiments, die mit schwarzen Schildern mit weissem Punkt ausgerüstet sind, tragen einen Gürtel aus Rindsleder. **H3** Die Uniform dieses Kriegers der uKhandempemvu unterscheidet sich von H2; er ist mit einem schwarzen Schild ausgestattet und trägt einen Federstutz an seinem Kopf. **H4** Ein *Udibi* Junge; sie wurden als Diener der jeweiligen Krieger beschäftigt.

I1 König Mpande kaSenzangakhoma tanzt mit seinen Kriegern (*ca.1870*). Die Kleidung des Königs für Feierlichkeiten setzte sich aus Affenfell und Kuhschwänzen zusammen. Seine Kopfbedeckung bestand aus weissen Straussen-, Lourie- und Kranichfedern. **I2** In den siebziger Jahren des vorigen Jahrhunderts hatten sich die Unterschiede der Uniformen der Regimenter verringert. Dieser umXapho Krieger trägt am gesamten Kopf Straussenfedern und ein schwarzes Schild. **I3** Das iNdlu-yengwe Regiment trug eine ähnliche Tracht wie I2. Der Unterschied lag jedoch in der Anordnung der Federn und den weissen Punkten auf der unteren Hälfte des Schilds.

J1 Der *isangoma* oder 'Wahrsager' spielte eine wichtige Rolle bei den Kriegsvorbereitungen. Er war durch sein geflochtenes Haar charakterisiert und trug Talisman-Anhänger an seinem Körper. **J2** Ein Krieger des iNgobamakhosi Regiments in seiner Kampfbekleidung aus Hörnern und ein rot-weisses Schild. **J3** Das Thulwana Regiment war ein Gegner der iNgobamakhosi; obbleich sie alle in Ulundi wohnten, bekämpften sie sich zu sehr, um zusammenzuleben.

K1 Dieser Krieger des Mbonambi Regiments trifft Vorbereitungen, um die rituelle Verstümmelung, die an den feindlichen Leichen nach der Schlacht vorgenommen wurde, durchzuführen. **K2** Die volle Uniform des iNdlondlo Regiments war bei weitem zu aufwendig, dass sie im Kampf getragen hätte werden können; deshalb ist dieser Krieger nur mit einem notwendigen Minimum versehen. **K3** Wie K2 trägt auch dieser iNgobamakhosi Krieger nur das absolut Nopwendige, ist aber in einem Uniformrock eines Soldaten der 24. Regiments gekleidet. Zahlreiche Hinterlader gerieten nach Isandlwana in die Hände der Zulu.

L1 Dieser Zulu Rebelle trug bei der Schlacht von Mhome Gorge abgelegte europäische Kleidung und das *ubushokobezi* Abzeichnen an seiner Kopfbedeckung. **L2** Die Durban Light Infantry trug Khakibekleidung für den Einsatz in den Tropen, die denen der britischen Verbände ähnlich war, wenngleich der Tropenhelm eine etwas andere Form annahm. **L3** Dieser Constable der Nogqayi gehörte der einheimischen Polizei von Zululand an und ist mit einem *Martini-Henry* Gewehr sowie schwarzer *Slade-Wallace* Austrüstung augestattet.